Responses to *The Auspicious You:* Letters to Hesitant and Hopeful Young Adults

—◦◦◦—

"I'm living through situations that Lori Vandeventer discusses in her letters. As I was reading, I had to stop multiple times, thinking Wow! How does she put the experience in such precise words of how things really are on campus? The letters are very reliable, and they have the potential to be life-changing for many young adults, myself included."

~Bailey Caswell, sophomore at Purdue University

"It's one thing to pick up a book and curl up with a cup of coffee when you need to relax. It's another to grab a book that has exactly what you need to hear written within its pages when life throws you another curveball. The letters within *The Auspicious You* are filled to the brim with love, care, and sometimes the strong words you need to get you back in action. There are a lot of obstacles in life, but *The Auspicious You* is a great tool to learn how to make the most out of every situation."

~Jason Childress, recent high school graduate on his way to Trine University

"As someone who has worked with students all over the country, I see how the transition to young adulthood and college is daunting and difficult. Lori Vandeventer not only puts into words the challenges all college students face, but she also gives practical and impactful advice. This book of letters is full of wisdom I wish I could share with every high school senior over a nice meal. Practical, authentic. Helpful."

~Michael Hartman, Youth Pastor at The Crossing, Windmill Campus, Las Vegas, Nevada

"Drawing from her own personal life stories as well as experience teaching and interacting with hundreds of youth, Lori Vandeventer has written a much-needed reference book for young people to utilize during one of the most challenging periods of their life. As a social worker who has had experience working with young people in both the school and private practice setting, I can testify one of the greatest questions they have is "who am I," apart from who everyone else has told me to be. Vandeventer's letters act as a guide, giving gentle yet direct advice and wisdom pointing young people in the direction of finding their true Auspicious You. I envision this book being valuable with individuals, in group settings, and in classroom instruction with students.

~Heather M. Hudson, Master of Social Work,
Licensed Clinical Social Worker

"Lori Vandeventer's writing style is just what students need. It's firm and to the point, but because her voice is so personal, students will connect to her and choose this book as a trusted resource. The stories included are very important, and there is a lesson in these letters for anyone who reads them."

~Jordyn Kieft, sophomore at Indiana University

THE AUSPICIOUS YOU

LETTERS TO HESITANT AND HOPEFUL YOUNG ADULTS

―⁓⁓―

LORI VANDEVENTER

Printed in the United States of America

Published by Author Academy Elite
P.O. Box 43, Powell, OH 43035
www.AuthorAcademyElite.com

Library of Congress Control Number: 2019906982

Paperback: 978-1-64085-716-2
Hardback: 978-1-64085-717-9
E-book: 978-1-64085-718-6

Available in paperback, hardback, e-book, and audiobook.
Interior book design by JetLaunch.
Cover design by Tri Widyatmaka through 99designs.
Author Pictures by Kevin Hudson, Hudson's Photography, Bedford, IN

www.lorivandeventer.com

Disclaimers

The author recreated events, locales, and conversations from her memories of them. In order to maintain their anonymity in some instances, she has changed the names of individuals and places, she may have changed some identifying characteristics and details such as physical properties, occupations, and places of residence.

Although the publisher and author have made every effort to ensure that the information in this book was correct at press time, the publisher and author do not assume and hereby disclaim any liability to any party for any loss, damage, or disruption caused by errors or omissions, whether such errors or omissions result from negligence, accident, or any other cause.

This book is not intended as a substitute for the advice of psychologists, counselors, or physicians. The reader should regularly consult a licensed professional in matters relating to his/her mental and physical health and particularly with respect to any symptoms that may require diagnosis or medical attention.

Any Internet addresses and telephone numbers printed in this book are offered as a resource. They are not intended in any way to be or imply an endorsement by the author or Author Academy Elite, nor does the author or Author Academy Elite vouch for the content of these sites and numbers for the life of this book.

Dedication

I've written this book to honor Sean and our children
Zachary and Megan
because they inspire me to chase dreams.

———

I've written this book for our siblings, nieces, nephews, their
spouses, and our Greats
because they are all worth every bit of effort.

———

I've written this book for my students
because their brave questions and trials and victories deserve
acknowledgement.

———

I've written this book to honor the blessings that God has
given me.

VanFamGroup

Be the sunshine.

———∞———

Table of Contents

Part 1
Relationships: Be friends but be aware.

Part Two
Stress: How do you eat an elephant?

Part Three
Encouragement: Be nice, do good things, make new friends!

Appendices
Information: Blessing Hearts

Preface

Auspicious is an adjective, and it describes you because you are a young adult who is interested in taming the stress in your life and making a positive impact on your family and friends. You are full of promise and are favorable, conducive to success, hopeful, optimistic, and encouraging. My auspicious reader, you have goals for your future, and you are excited to get through the difficult aspects of a young adult life to live fully and make a difference in the world.

Even though you are an auspicious young adult, you can hesitate and feel the uncertainty of interpersonal relationships as well as the stress and anxiety about making choices concerning your life and future. Hopeful readers can gain important insights from my letters and learn about fulfillment beyond making money in a career. You will benefit from my letters as you learn to focus on your ability to serve others and influence the world.

Also, your adult mentors and coaches will benefit from my letters because they can depend on help and leadership from my experience as a veteran teacher. My letters and the questions I provide will build confidence for mentors to prepare open discussions and lessons to lead you through these challenging subjects.

What can you expect from *The Auspicious You?*

- Three sections of top concerns for young adults: Relationships, Stress, and Encouragement.
- A format for you to progress page-by-page through each of the three thematic sections or to quickly turn to a specific letter, timely meeting a need.
- Authentic stories and frank discussion within each letter, encouraging you to turn away from drama and focus on the truth of situations.
- A consistent framework for each letter with space to explore your thoughts about identity, core beliefs, and service.

Are you ready to discover more of your auspicious self?

Introduction

I was an accident.

Literally. My parents were told that they couldn't have more children. When I was born, my sisters were sixteen and thirteen years old, and my arrival changed the dynamic of our family. I know that I added many challenges for my parents as they were older when I came along. Actually, my dad used to say that he wouldn't give a nickel for another one, but he wouldn't take a million for me. I'm still not sure how that makes me feel, even though I know he meant the teasing words as a loving affirmation.

Growing up in a small, southern Indiana town surrounded by my parents, sisters, family members, and all their friends gave me a strong sense of myself and a personal belief that I belong in a different generation. My parents lived through the Great Depression, and my sisters are Baby Boomers. I have assimilated the characteristics from those generations into my own, which blessed me with the most amazing childhood and the ability to give advice. No, more than that. I have a very bossy personality with a knack for somehow getting my advice to others right more often than I get it wrong. I'm lucky that a smidge of my parents' wisdom rubbed off on me. Bossing and serving are in my DNA, but at first, I didn't see these traits as a gift or talent. Then, one event changed me forever.

I remember one night after both of my sisters were married and out on their own. The big bedroom was finally mine, and I was allowed to pick out new curtains and bedspread. For some unknown reason, I picked a brown and orange color scheme, which still makes me shake my head and wonder about my decorating choices. Anyway, as I lay under the Halloweenish geometric patterns of the blanket, I could not sleep because my mind jumped from one idea to the next. I didn't have a conscious method in mind, but I vividly know that I spent most of the night with my heart racing and my excitement building as I made plans to babysit, serve as a counselor at a youth camp, and teach in my own classroom. At the time, I wasn't old enough to do any of these activities, but I knew for certain my future was set at that moment.

Even with such a specific experience to help direct my decisions, I can report that my life was still filled with mountains and valleys. The end of high school was interesting, and my first year of college proved to be one of the most miserable times I've ever endured, but you'll find out more about my homesickness later. For now, I want you to know that even bossy people who think they know what they are doing in life don't really have a clue. Every one of us must struggle and juggle internal and external pressures while trying to make the difficult leap from one stage of life to another.

My personal and professional experiences have solidified my belief that all humans have the potential to make an impact in their circle of influence when they take an interest in continual growth and development. How do you feel about your potential? As a young adult, you are standing at the precipice of a wide-open future for you to make your own. Young people amaze me with their desire to learn and grow;

they want to set and meet their goals to improve the world around us. I love that! Since you are showing love and care for yourself by reading my letters dealing with relationships, stress, and encouragement, I know you have the same spirit that favors success and promise in your future! The book in your hands has been in production for dozens of years in my heart. I have shared these words with countless students before you who have met their challenges with courage and peace.

There's no real trick to moving through the letters I've written to you. You can read the letters in order, and you will see a progression of personal development for you to follow. However, you can also jump from one letter to another, reading just the right one at just the right time to meet the needs of your life in the moment. You will be able to read the letters over and over, gaining new insight with each new reading because as you grow and change, a new piece of advice will stand out to you. My best instruction, though, is to read one letter at a time. Each one provides a fair amount of information, and you will be more successful making a lasting change if you spend time with each letter and refrain from moving through them too quickly.

I've also given you space at the end of each letter to spend some time with yourself and your thoughts. You can doodle, draw a chart or graph, journal, and record ideas to help you internalize the advice in my letter and decide how to put it into practice in your life. The letters are also awesome discussion starters for you to share with others. You'll be amazed at how much you can learn from other students your age as well as your parents and mentors when you ask genuine questions and search for valid answers together.

My sincere desire to serve you started as a small spark on that sleepless night so many years ago when I felt the need and the calling to work with students. That dream came true for me, and I've been training to write this book for most of my adult life. Through these pages, an *Auspicious You* will also figure out how to make your own dreams come true.

Blessings to you!

—~~~—

PART 1

Relationships

Be friends but be aware.

We might as well jump right into the deep end with relationships. Your connections to other people should be one of the most important parts of your life. These connections develop your pathos, the ability to feel compassion, because of the emotions and feelings you have in your heart. While young adults are historically considered very self-centric, by the time you are a high school upperclassman or a beginning college student, you are very interested in improving and investing in relationships with others.

By this age, most of you have been hurt by a broken heart delivered from an ex-best friend or a romantic relationship that ended. Your young hearts have conflicted feelings of needing and demanding independence while also desperately wanting to know that your families and support systems are firmly in place as you make life-changing decisions about the future. These letters will focus on the heart of relationship successes and failures while also showing you how to stay grounded in truth and a healthy perspective.

—⚬⚬⚬—

Ready, Set, Decide!

Dear Auspicious You,

True Story. I watched two different young women, at two different times, absolutely fall apart because their whole plan for their futures had come into question. Even though these events occurred a couple of years apart, I'm joining the details here for you. You need to see that you are not alone when you become hesitant and wonder which decision to make as you balance the relationships you've built with mentors. Hearing about these stories should give you strength to listen to your own voice, even if you don't think your unique voice is very confident or loud.

Both of these ladies showed promise in the classroom, had great GPA's and super fun personalities, sincerely wanted to make a difference in other lives, and developed a plan to begin the next chapter of their journey based on their own desires. Sadly, both ended up in tears. Instead of trusting their own research and plans, they each allowed someone else to change their focus and create doubt in their minds about their future decisions. I watched and was amazed as one scrambled to apply to a new university and the other to change her intended major. Seriously, the girls reminded me of cartoon characters who were shuffling papers and trying to run with wheels for legs, but absolutely going nowhere. I couldn't get either one of these very smart and usually collected young women to calm down enough to even talk to me about what happened to upset them.

After I listened to a long explanation from one of the girls and traded several crazy long emails with the other, I uncovered the truth of the situations. Basically, they were each scared of making a big mistake about their future. In each case, a well-meaning and trusted adult rather forcefully imparted a different opinion about what each girl *should* do. A reliable mentor, with a very strong voice, cast doubt over these huge life decisions. I would have been freaked out, too. Can you imagine thinking that you have your whole plan set and then someone that you depend on for advice doesn't just crack open a small fissure of doubt, but creates a whole canyon of questions?

Ok, let's stop for a minute. What would you do here? Since you are calmly reading and feeling safe right now, you might be thinking that either I'm exaggerating or that you wouldn't let someone else affect you so strongly. Surely, the girls in the story didn't react so strongly, and if they did, maybe their sense of self wasn't solidly intact. Right? I'm not using my gift of hyperbole here. If you haven't felt this pressure from a trusted voice, try to relate for a minute.

What is the plan for your future? Where do you see yourself in the next years? Do you have a solid, I-know-for-sure feeling about your choices? If you are being totally honest and totally mature about these questions, you will admit that although you have a plan, you are wise enough to know that life can happen and change up the details for you. But what will you do if someone in your inner circle of relationships tries to change the details for you?

If you are a star athlete in your high school, are you getting recruited by anyone? Division I, II, or III? Junior college or a four-year university? Are you good enough to compete in a premier school? Does the school who wants you actually have a degree program that fits with your future goals? I have watched athletes struggle with these questions for years. I can assure you that the next level of competition in your sport will be different from your current experience. When you finally make your decision and make your verbal commitment, are you ready for the loads of "advice" you will get from everyone? If you choose a DIII school because you truly feel at home on campus and you know the degree curriculum is exactly what you want to do, how will you handle the well-meaning family members who have a higher opinion of your ability than anyone else? When they begin to get in your head with comments about DI or DII and start questioning you for choosing a DIII, what will you do?

Maybe your family struggles financially. Maybe you are the child in the family who takes care of the younger siblings when your parents can't—or won't because they are more than happy to let you make a meal, do laundry, and help with homework. Perhaps you have a single-parent family, and your responsibility to your loved ones is simply how you all make life work. Or, possibly, you have one of the famous helicopter parents who has taken care of every detail of your life so far including schedules, choosing courses to take, and budgeting money.

Every person who comes through high school and moves into a post-secondary educational setting has a different background, an individual story. You are no different. The one huge similarity comes from your excitement and anxiousness about the future. Another way that all continuing students resemble each other comes from the second-guessing because of well-meaning and trusted adults. You will have to take steps to protect your relationship with your mentors as well as protect and develop your own adult persona. You will know in your heart which decision you want to make.

I can share a secret with you at this point. Honestly, no decision about your future can mess you up so much that your life will be over before it begins. (Obviously, I'm talking about selecting a school, major, dorm or apartment, etc. You are smart enough to know that plenty of harmful decisions will put you and others at risk.) If you decide to go to school A, and the campus isn't a good fit for you, will you switch to school B after a semester is completed? If you realize that you've let someone's opinion affect you so much that you change your plans, get back on track as soon as possible. My hope is that you will see you are not alone in feeling insecure about your future plan, which should give you courage.

Take that courage and trust your own voice. This might sound harsh, but if someone continues to push you down or dictate your choices, you must recognize the actions or words as manipulative and then move forward without feeling guilty about not doing what someone else says (even if you have a close relationship with that someone). You've listened to and obeyed your respected elders for the entirety of your life up until now. As you prepare to take the next steps into adulthood, be ready to make your own decisions and then accept both the benefits and the consequences of those decisions.

For example, I know that your heart is in the right place when you want to stay and take care of younger siblings, but that's not your job, even if a parent makes you feel responsible. If you truly want to change the trajectory of your whole family, seek more education. Go to college or a trade school. Secure the apprenticeship. If you show your younger siblings the way out of a dysfunctional home or away from manipulative comments from loved ones, then you are providing the best gift that you can give. Blaze that trail!

As you make and then stand up for your own choices, you might have to cut ties with certain people. Or, you might just have to smile and thank the advice-giver as you take ideas into consideration and then act on your own, adult decision.

Either way, stay focused on your end goal. You can be respectful to others and honor your own life at the same time by following these steps:

- Recognize that most people who want to make decisions for you are trying to help. However, as a young adult who is maturing and moving into the next step of life, you must make these decisions for yourself.
- Soak up every bit of advice from the adults and mentors around you. Instead of becoming anxious about their suggestions, weigh their opinions in your mind and heart. Be attentive and ask questions.
- Develop methods to chart the suggestions and options given by your mentors so that you can visually see the various elements of your decision, both positive and negative. Run the statistics of success rates versus failure rates with any decision that allows for numbers. Create a positive/negative chart to show the good/bad implications of each option.
- When you have all the information, settle in a quiet place by yourself. Meditate. Visualize yourself meeting your goals. Figure out which decision provides you with the most peace.

Then, YOU make YOUR personal decision.

In the end, the peace in your heart will assure you that you made the right choice. Remember the girls that I mentioned at the beginning? Eventually, they each calmed down and took time to process the options and implications of changing their decisions as a result of someone else. Neither girl ended up changing her school or major. But, the added research and soul-searching helped them make informed decisions which led to valuable degrees and careers. You will do the same. When you are faced with a dilemma of choices and varied pieces of advice from different mentors who have all proven helpful in the past, move through the process and make an informed decision that leaves you with a peace in your heart.

—⁓⁓⁓—

Reflection

- What decision do you currently face?
- What are your thoughts?
- What pressures or external advice are you receiving?
- Does this advice support or negate your personal decision?
- Do you truly trust the people who are encouraging you or placing doubts in your mind?
- Are the suggestions increasing your stress or your assurance?
- Which option gives you a sense of peace in your heart?

—⁓⁓⁓—

Your Space

Fluid Friendships

Dear Auspicious You,

ook at your kindergarten self. In your mind's eye, visualize a picture of yourself during this time. Do you have your front teeth? Are you wearing an amazing outfit that you picked out all by yourself? Does your hairstyle scream bed head or sweet cut and curls? Even if life was hard at that time, can you still see the hope and innocence? Pretty cute, aren't you?

What about the 7th grade you? What do you see when you study your own face at that age? Braces? A smile that hides how hard you are trying to fit in to the group at the lunch table? Too much makeup? Chubby cheeks? A kid who made mean comments to someone just so that you'd feel stronger? Bright eyes still glowing from the freshness of summer camp that changed your life? Lips that just received a first kiss?

Now, study the sophomore version of you. That was a hard year, wasn't it? You weren't quite old enough to drive or be an upperclassman, but you were definitely not a baby anymore. This age of being somewhere in between is so difficult. What do your eyes reveal here? Can you see the insecurity edging its way into your mind? Maybe the picture you remember was taken right before a major change in your life. You had more freedom at that point, but did you use it wisely? Can you see a reflection of a choice that you felt old enough to make at the time? Can you see the hints of concern because you knew that you were placing yourself in situations where you didn't feel comfortable so that you wouldn't be left out? Still, does the set of your jaw stand out to you? Does it show that you were developing a determination to set your own goals and find your own independence?

How many hours would it take for you to explain how you have changed from kindergarten to 7th grade to 10th grade to now?

———

Guess what? You are not the only person in your class who faced such changes. At the time, your psychological development was geared to be concerned mostly about your own life, but each and every friend and classmate was going through these same changes. It's no wonder that your friendships are fluid as you pass from one stage into the next.

Personally, I know as I grew during these years, I was very self-centered. Don't get me wrong. I loved to help other people and, as I shared earlier, my personal revelation for my whole future calling happened right in the middle of this timeline, but I still focused on me. I didn't have the maturity to see how my words and actions affected others even though I thought I did. As I grew and changed, my friend group changed, too. I had several best friends through this time.

In elementary school, one girl and I were very close, and we were able to spend many days each week together. Then, as we each branched out into new activities and groups, our friendship changed. Sadly, we barely talked during middle school and high school. During the middle years, another girl and I spent countless hours and family vacation trips and phone conversations and sleepovers together. We were blessed to have shared our sets of parents with each other as extended supporters. She was like a sister and an integral part of my childhood and life, and I will always love her dearly. However, we also grew apart as we grew up and into our own interests and roles. As an upperclassman in high school, my activities again created opportunities for me to be with certain people who became my close friends and confidants. Not too far into college, people I didn't even know six months before were suddenly a part of my inner-circle.

For a long time as my friend group changed, I suffered from the loss. At first, I blamed the people I lost because I didn't want to accept any responsibility for our drifting apart. Then, I transitioned into feeling guilty because I figured my selfishness and bossy personality compounded our separation and caused problems that made me grow apart from my friends. I then felt I was the only one at fault, but I was not brave enough or mature enough to share those feelings with anyone. In fact, out loud, I continued to blame others and various situations so that I felt better about myself. Let me tell you, that didn't work out well for me. I lost touch with these past friends for far too long just because of my attitude. I didn't recognize any of this when I was living in the middle of it.

As a teacher, I watched my students going through the same types of friend group evolution, which taught me so much. Now, I know that even though I was focused on my own life and interests, my friendships were going to change anyway. I don't see students enter and leave these different stages of life with the same friends. Apparently, friendships grow and cycle through many seasons as a normal and healthy process.

None of us should take these changes personally. Luckily, I have reconnected with these girls from my childhood, and we still share a priceless past and present. Your various friendships will also change and grow individually. You might keep the same friends from your elementary years as you add others when your experiences expand, or you might find the relationships cycling through fluctuations like mine.

Where are you in this process? I hope you take an educated look at the changes in your friend group. I would love for you to see that as you all matured from the adorable kindergarteners to the wise people you are now, your friendships changed, too. Now, as you visualize the pictures of you in the different stages, broaden your view to also include your friends. How have you all developed and changed?

A while ago, one young girl named Clara seemed like she was on top of the world. She was a good athlete and student, friendly, and pretty, and she was solidly placed inside of the "popular" group in school. The problem was the drama within this group almost pushed her over the edge. The people in the friend group would talk about each other, stir drama, and misuse all the forms of social media that adults always warn kids to avoid. The manipulation and bullying were strong within the group as well as from the group to other students. Anyone who threatened their sense of power or who created even the smallest bit of jealousy in their hearts became targets.

Teachers and other adults didn't easily see the problem because these kids were experts at turning on and off the mean streaks at will. Some of the parents even added to the stress as they posted pictures and their own brand of manipulation online for the whole world to see. The stress became so overwhelming for Clara that she literally sought refuge in a classroom during lunch. She ate in the room, by herself, for several days before anyone noticed. During this time, she knew she had to separate from this group because she could no longer stand the gossip and the verbal arrows they were shooting. Still, the tension between having a group, even a snotty one, and being alone or finding a new group was overwhelming. Eventually, Clara found her balance again.

Another set of people who were also past members and targets of the mean bunch opened lines of communication with her. She found a new lunch table and a new sense of independence. Now, Clara can look outside of herself and notice when other people are in the predicament that she faced. Like the friendly face who offered her a way to re-establish herself, she now offers the same to others. Yes, Clara lost the friends in the first group, but look at how she grew. Just as you changed from 7th grade to 10th grade, Clara also transformed and needed to update her friends to create equilibrium in her life again.

Clara's story shows that some groups change on purpose as you get kicked to the curb or as you join or remove yourself based on your own intentions. If you feel like you have been ditched by your best friends and don't understand why, take a serious look at your behavior. Do you demand to be the one in control of everyone or at the center of attention? Do you start the gossip and the drama? Do you promise to be a reliable friend but then leave the group as soon as a "better" invitation comes along?

Seriously consider your role and responsibility for how the group has excluded you. Absolutely no one is perfect, so like me, you will find behaviors and personality traits that may have prompted (or caused) the group to pick you as the next one out. However, you should also look at the other people in the group. Like Clara, you might find yourself on the outside looking in and wondering what happened. I promise other people who care about you are also wondering, so I suggest talking to them about the situation. You probably know some caring adults who can be amazingly awesome to just listen without trying to fix anything when you tell them you just need a shoulder and a trustworthy ear as you share the story out loud. I find moments of clarity happen when I talk through an issue because I think out loud. You might be the same.

If you realize you need to apologize for your own poor behavior, do it. Be brave and set a time and talk face-to-face so you can clear the air. You don't have to continue being friends, but you owe it to them and to yourself to own your part of the problem.

However, if you realize you aren't comfortable with the type of language or the manipulation or the gossip coming from someone else, then they might be targeting you because you make the others more aware of how they are behaving poorly. Honestly, it's better to enjoy your own company instead of hooking your wagon to a group that makes bad choices. Drinking, drugs, sexual activity, skipping school, ditching homework, bullying, and manipulating others are all absolute red flags and should make you want to leave a friend group without looking back.

You can still be nice to the people in that group. Be respectful to them, don't gossip about them, and say hello when you see them. Be friends but be aware. You don't have to tell them your whole story anymore. You don't have to stay and listen while feeling uncomfortable about the conversations. You can be polite and friendly without being sucked into the middle of the drama.

If you find yourself compromising your morals and personal standards just to be part of a group, then be alone. I know how awful that sounds. I know the social implications that happen because of what I'm suggesting. I've lived through them. During my college years, I spent most of my time alone because I didn't drink or smoke. I went to class and to my two jobs. I studied and made my grades a priority because that was the only way to keep my scholarship money and stay in school. If I had it to do over again, I would probably make the same choice. Granted, I was lonely and often wondered if I missed out on the true "college experience," but then I think about the times I did try to fit in with others. The smells and the talk and the scenes running through my memory remind me why I made my choices. I was able to have acquaintances in all areas of my life while staying in control of myself.

But what if I would have branched out and looked for new people who felt the same way I did? Now, many years into my life, I absolutely love the adventure of meeting new people. I have learned how an exercise class, a volunteer opportunity, a new co-worker, or a new church group will offer me the opportunity to interact with others. From those interactions, I can watch friendships develop into many different types from colleagues to true inner-circle people who share my life as I share in theirs.

I don't think I was ready for that kind of searching when I was in college, but I sure wish I could go back and talk to my 20-year-old self about relationships. I'd give myself the same pep-talk I'm giving you now. I'd tell myself to recognize friendships are fluid, and that's ok. Then, I'd encourage myself to tear down my wall a bit so I could at least try to explore this type of maturity in finding friends. I'd remind myself that few seconds of insane courage can change your life.[1]

Does any of this sound familiar? Has your best friend changed as you moved from one stage of life to another? Have you allowed yourself to stay in a friend group even when you know you should move along? Have you taken the brave steps of growing up and out? Basically, that's the basis of this whole conversation.

As you grow and mature, your relationships with friends should do the same. When you feel at ease with your friends and your own conscience, you can have the best times of your life. You can laugh, cry, rant, dance, sing, and rest together. You will find support when you need it as well as the exact kind of support you need. You will find the people who know what you are thinking by the look on your face and who answer with the look on their faces. These friends offer safety and comfort. When you have found yourself wondering about your choice of friends, take the next step into maturity and realistically look at the situation.

—✎—

Reflection

- Have you pulled away from someone? Why?
- Has someone pulled away from you? Why?
- Has a new step in life (joining a sport, club, or activity; scheduling classes for your interests; starting a new job) allowed/forced you to find a new friend?
- Are you comfortable and happy in your own skin while you are with this friend or group?
- What does the friend/group do that makes you proud to be associated with them?
- Do you silently cringe at anything that is said or done by the friend/group? Why?
- What responsibility do you carry in creating an issue with your friends?
- Have you looked for new friends in productive ways? What other methods can you use to open yourself to new friendships?

—✎—

Your Space

High Maintenance

Dear Auspicious You,

I think I should apologize before I begin this letter, or at least caution you because I might offend some people with this one. My belief system here appears to be a bit, no...a bunch...judgmental and based on appearance. I completely understand this letter will put me at risk for writing a hasty generalization. (That's a logical fallacy where the writer creates a problem because she pigeonholes all members of a group into one category based on the behavior of a few people. Yes, I'm an English teacher. Yes, I just took advantage of making sure you knew the rhetorical term.)

Still, I'm going to write it. I feel that strongly about this subject. I know not all people who look a certain way behave in a certain way, but I need to share this information in the most authentic voice possible. This is how I explain it to the young people in my daily life, so this is how I'll explain it to you. Don't get angry if I'm describing you.

Some people need more attention than others, and if they don't receive attention, they create problems. Like many others, I call this being high maintenance. I've tried to teach my own children to not be high maintenance and to recognize the sight of it and run in the opposite direction. Run fast. High maintenance can describe a hobby (such as gardening), a pet, your friend, or a significant other. For what you need to know about relationships, we won't worry about the tomato plants or the puddle-making puppy. I want to share with you about high maintenance people and how relationships are strained because of this trait.

You know the type. You've seen the guy who checks himself out in every mirror or window reflection, flexing just a bit to make sure the muscle is still there, adjusting the hair spike just so. I'm sure you've noticed the girl who wears all the makeup, needs the brand name clothes, purchases and flaunts the top fashion items from the sunglasses perched on top of her head down to her shoes. Underneath the beautiful-people exterior, these folks have a need to be in the spotlight. They are loud, demanding. If everyone in the room isn't paying enough attention to them, they create a dialogue or a scene to make sure their needs are met to their satisfaction.

A high maintenance friend won't let you make decisions about activities and will always need to be in control. She will love and gush all over you if you are willing to keep her firmly placed at the top of the pedestal of your friendship. He will hang out with you when it's convenient for him, but will also dump you if a more interesting, high profile invitation comes along. When it comes to true connections and vulnerability, a high maintenance person's walls are sky-high. She won't let you see any struggle and covers with a plastic exterior, loudly proclaiming all is well and life couldn't be better. It's annoying, isn't it? I mean, who does that?

Honestly? Sometimes I do. And, you probably do, too. Everyone has the ability and/or the history of being high maintenance at times. I know when I've done it, and I feel awful about the situation. Being high maintenance, however, is more than showing an arrogant or tough exterior to cover up insecurity. It's also more than having an affinity for expensive items or being needy.

The trouble comes when you feel control over your situation slipping from you, so you bump up the type-A-ness of yourself to reestablish control. Many times, jealousy is the catalyst. Maybe someone else is getting the attention you think you deserve for a job well planned and executed. Maybe your friend is spending more time with someone else, so you make a big production out of a budding friendship just to keep up, but when the old friend asks for a night together, you dump the new one. Have you noticed some of these tendencies in yourself? Do you know how to deal with the problems effectively? How can you grow and mature?

First, congratulate yourself for recognizing these traits in your own behavior. Now you can be aware and guard yourself against being high maintenance. When you see these tendencies in yourself, you can get to the root of the problem for you. Why do you feel the need to be in control and in the center of attention? Do you need the affirmation because of a shaky self-perception? Are you a control freak who thinks your ideas are superior to all others? Do you get jealous of other people when they succeed? All these issues are common and a normal part of moving through life's growing pains. When you privately assess your behavior, you will recognize your own triggers.

If you are ready for your immature adolescent self to emerge as an adult, pursue ways to turn your selfishness into generosity. If this is the case for you, open your eyes to the gifts and talents of the people around you. Be happy for someone else's successes and celebrate them! Too often, we are all pitted against each other because of a crazy sense of competition. If another girl looks pretty, you feel threatened, so you don't like her. No! If another girl looks pretty, you should tell her! Give a compliment and get ready for a mind shift. Instead of tearing down someone else because he appears to be having a better day than you, let yourself admire him. Call out your envy and do away with it. Empower each of you when you share your admiration out loud.

I know you've heard this before, but I still don't see people truly embracing the power of positivity. Smile. Give compliments. Perform an act of random kindness. When you give a bit of yourself away in a positive manner, your day improves. Your attitude improves. The absolute key to never falling into a high maintenance role again stems from serving others.

I know other factors that make you high maintenance can come from deeper hurts: physical and mental abuse from someone you trusted, being truly abandoned by someone who should have taken care of you, or suffering the tragedy of another loss. If this level of hurt has happened to you, you might feel you have every right to be demanding and protective of yourself. You are in the middle of some important work while you process the injuries done to you, and as you walk through recovering from these deep wounds, you *will* need extra attention and support. Your inner-circle of trusted adults, counselors, friends, and family need to help you sort out your emotions and help you make the best decisions to move forward.

Still, during this process, you can serve others. As you feel able, you can give compliments, smile, and offer to share your story to connect with another person who might also be suffering. Allowing yourself to be vulnerable in this way will most definitely be scary, but the benefits of connecting to others instead of hiding behind a persona of a certain "look" or attitude will help you heal. You will find peace and support when you feel like you are making a difference for someone else. Your story is important and might be the exact encouragement someone else needs to survive their own trials.

You can control your own high maintenance, but what about the tendencies of others? How have you been impacted by another person who demands attention? You have options:

run in the opposite direction to not get sucked into the misery or be friends but be aware. You can only control your own behavior and attitude. If a friend is high maintenance, you can still be friends and enjoy time together.

However, as you are aware of his tendencies, you shouldn't get mad at him if you place yourself in a situation with him. By being friends, you can share a conversation or do homework together, but when he starts pressuring you to follow along while he behaves in ways you don't like, you must act for you. Politely remove yourself from the situation. You can share your concerns and initiate an open conversation explaining why you are uncomfortable. You might open his eyes to a new way of thinking, but you might also make him angry when you call him out on his poor behavior. Either way, reserve your emotion and remove yourself from him.

If you know a girl is needy, demanding, and bossy, don't pursue a relationship with her. Be nice, give a compliment, smile. Don't ask her out on a date. In the beginning, you will like her confidence and the look of a well-dressed beauty. But what's underneath the skin? If she isn't nice to other girls, if she isn't friendly to your friends, if she demands your time with no concern for your siblings, then what's the benefit? Seriously, go the other direction. Be nice, give a compliment, smile. Run the other way. You will save yourself a pile of heartache in the end.

No future relationship will end well when the prospective partner is demanding and controlling, no matter how cute he or she might be. Plus, if you allow yourself to become entangled with a high maintenance significant other, you will find that type of person very hard to leave. Getting away from a bad relationship is difficult enough, but when you partner yourself with someone you know to be controlling, the endings are even more painful.

I am so proud of the work you are doing with this tough topic. High maintenance tendencies are in all of us to a certain extent, and I am sure you will continue to investigate yourself to locate the reasons these tendencies appear in you and in the people around you. Once you recognize them, you can isolate the causes and commit to removing the behavior, or the high maintenance person, from your life. You will be much more satisfied with your relationships when you empower others as well as yourself.

———〰〰〰———

Reflection

- What makes you high maintenance?
- How will you combat this tendency?
- How do you unproductively react to others who are high maintenance?
- How can you effectively respond to others who are high maintenance?

———〰〰〰———

Your Space

Don't Send the Text (or the Picture) Because STDs Are Real

Dear Auspicious You,

Once upon a time, a young man named Bob walked into class without a pencil. He had no idea such an insignificant mistake would rock his world that day. This guy wasn't a troublemaker, even though he did get mouthy with a couple of teachers when he was younger. He knew the importance of getting his diploma, and he could visualize himself in a job, making money to support himself. He was excited about his future, even though he didn't talk about it with any of the adults around him.

Bob arrived as the class started. The instructor dove into the lecture, and Bob started rummaging through his backpack, searching for a pencil. As the lecture continued, Bob kept zipping and unzipping different compartments, becoming more frustrated with himself because he couldn't find his pencil. Finally, the instructor stopped talking and just stared at Bob.

Suddenly, every eye in the room focused squarely on him and his fumbling. He stopped and looked back at the teacher. He could feel his cheeks warming and his heart beating faster because of this unwanted attention. The teacher asked if he had a problem causing him to be so disruptive during lecture. Bob tried to explain about his lost pencil, but the teacher cut him off mid-sentence.

In a typical classroom, the teacher would have just given Bob a pencil and moved on with class, but that's not what happened in this tale. The instructor berated Bob, asking why he didn't have a pencil, saying he should get a job to buy supplies, and pointing out that Bob was a subpar student because he didn't come prepared to class. Bob heard all he cared to hear. He got up from his desk with the intention of leaving the room.

In the silence of a tense classroom, dozens of eyes watched him. The teacher confronted him and said he was not allowed to walk away from the situation because he should stand up and solve the problem like a man. That was the last straw. Bob turned on the teacher and angrily roared at him using words he would later regret. He felt insulted and pushed the teacher out of the way, so he could leave the room. The shove was stronger than Bob intended, and the teacher lost his balance and fell, cracking his head on the edge of the desk and then the floor. Blood pooled under him.

Students in the room sprang to action as some restrained Bob and others attended to the instructor. Someone called for help, and the school's resource officer arrived. He handcuffed Bob. Bob was thoroughly confused and kept muttering something about a pencil as he was led away to the police car.

This fictitious story might seem far-fetched to you, but have you been in a situation where the tension and the consequences became serious very quickly? When a situation escalates in a hostile or antagonistic manner, you might have exclaimed, "Whoa! That just got real!" For young people, peer pressure plus a brain that isn't fully developed to think through long-term consequences create a very bad combination. Unchecked emotions cause impulses to do and say what you normally wouldn't, and impulses cause many regrets. The saddest part about the real-life situations I see regularly comes from social media platforms making these impulses very, very public.

As a young adult, you KNOW all the warnings about social media and texting. You have probably been impacted negatively because of a chaotic technology mess. So why am I even writing this letter to you if you already know? That's the million-dollar question. Young adults live through one tech crisis and then jump into another, and I can't figure out why.

You tell me.

Here's what I do know. Once a message is sent, your published words are one misplaced copy-and-paste away from becoming the next meme or virtual punching bag. Even if you are sending the message to your best friend, you put yourself at risk with the printed word. (Remember my letter about Fluid Friendships?) Is a text worth this risk?

I know you face situations that make your blood boil. I do, too. I know you want to support and defend the people close to you. I do, too. In the time we've been married, my husband has publicly served as a varsity basketball coach and a high school principal. I have gone through a long hiatus from social media because of posts that were sometimes passively aggressive and sometimes openly directed at my husband. My gut wrenched, and I wanted to post and defend my husband. In those moments, I had to refocus my attention and remember all the people who shared my husband's vision. I looked to the blessings in our lives and made myself thankful for the people who supported us and loved us. I realized my shift in attention created peace inside of me so I could let the negative comments evaporate.

My desire for you is the same. Look to the positive. Find the blessings. When you are tempted to get caught up in a game of social media verbal tag, pause. You must think through why you want to respond to a text or a social media post, especially when you are emotional. The first experts to discuss social media explained how the technology allowed young people to respond to others and to communicate messages they would never vocalize in person. I still believe this is true.

However, I see an even bigger problem now. Not only are young adults bolstered with the veil of technology, but they are also more impacted by the addiction to technology than they realize. Am I describing you? I witness people who simply cannot put down their phones. After a standardized test session where all phones were put away on my desk, students were anxious to get them back. As the last students finished, another teacher came in the room to converse with me about testing procedures. While we were obviously talking about testing, I had multiple students interrupt us by literally pulling on my arm and sleeve asking for their phones. These 17-year-old students couldn't wait another five minutes. The whole scene makes me sad and angry all at the same time.

You can search for yourself and learn how apps and social media sites use various algorithms to manipulate you. You can locate one study after another explaining how technology physically changes your brain and manipulates you.[2] I don't have the space or expertise to delve into those issues in my letter to you, but I do have the passion to encourage you to find out the truth for yourself. Don't be manipulated and controlled by the phone in your hand. Knowing the technology in place isn't innocently waiting to serve you, but rather purposefully manipulating you, I hope you see the dangers involved with your phone.

Even more, I want you to see the danger coming your way when you use the phone for an emotional response.

When a text or post makes you emotional, step away for a minute. Stop thinking you must answer every text immediately. Even polite people behave rudely when they interrupt a face-to-face conversation to check their phone or respond to someone. Let it beep or chime or ding without jumping for the phone like Pavlov's dog. Practice untethering yourself from your phone every day, so you can break away from the manipulation and brain changes your phone creates. With everyday messages, wait to respond. Finish what you are doing instead of leaping into texting action. Notice how controlling the impulses dealing with benign situations will also help you control your actions when larger consequences are at stake.

Have you broken up with someone only to have the person text and message you on multiple social media formats without stopping? Many relationships have ended badly because one person continually sent texts and social media posts. I've known several rough break ups where one person started texting and messaging the lost love's friends, demanding that they make the person respond. Really?

If you were calm and using logic instead of emotion, would you think this makes sense? If you and your significant other break up, then don't communicate by text or social media. Talk out the problem in person and then be done. If you are the dumped one, the worst action you can take is smothering the other person. Your ex will realize the decision to break up with you was the right one because of your needy and pushy messages. If you are the one receiving the pleading messages, block your ex. If the attempts to contact you continue, tell a trusted adult.

Whatever you do, whether you are communicating with a past significant other or a friend or an enemy, take a breath from the emotion. Do not respond with mean and angry words, even if you feel the words are justified. Deal with your emotion first, and then you can calmly figure out how to handle the situation. Sending a text filled with bitter and mean words isn't the answer because those words can be saved with a screen shot and then shared repeatedly. Don't present yourself in that way.

Maybe you deal well with negative emotions from social media and know how to step away. What about other emotions? Teasing, flirting, excitement, and being hyped up can get you in just as much of a mess. You might be messaging a boyfriend or girlfriend using social media or texting, and in this relationship, you might feel completely protected and comfortable. The two of you may share a complete trust, so you don't guard yourselves with private messages. What happens when her mom checks her phone? Maybe his younger sibling uses his phone and gets mixed up in the messages inadvertently. What happens when you both change and break up? Those texts and messages are still available. Pictures are still saved. My heart hurts for the ones who have made this mistake. Think before you text. And, no matter what, do not send an inappropriate picture. Honestly, don't even take the picture in the first place.

I don't care if you're in love.

I don't care if you're afraid to be called out as a coward.

I don't care if you lost a bet and feel the need to pay up.

I don't care if someone sent you one first.

I don't care if you've been promised a modeling contract for it.

Think logically right now in the calm of reading my letter. You know this. No good can come from sending emotionally charged words or pictures, releasing the content into the world for anyone to screen shot and send on to someone else. Decisions about the way you defend a family member, the personal and private details of your relationship with a significant other, or your physical sexuality should never be broadcast to the world. Make the adult decision to protect yourself and the ones you care about when it comes to texting and social media.

I've seen enough distress with the young people in my life over the years to know decisions to post and send sexual content have real consequences. Strong emotional troubles come with people seeing your sexting content. You can become the target of the gossip and bullying, and relationships will most likely end. You will take direct hits with shame, humiliation, and regret.

Along with these personal trials, you could also have public and legal penalties.[3] You need to educate yourself by researching the current laws in your area because young adults who participate in sexting can end up with possible pornography charges. They might have to register as sex offenders, and their parents can also possibly be in legal trouble because of their actions. Even if both parties are of age, please think and hesitate. Sexually transmitted diseases exist. Sometimes students' sexting is a catalyst for hooking up with someone. I know true stories of young adults who have an STD, but who still search for another partner. Those kinds of outcomes are simply too much high-risk for any coy message or post.

Remember the story at the beginning of my letter? Bob simply forgot his pencil, but he ended up arrested for assaulting his instructor. You might want to spout off to someone online which could result in a real-life fight, or you might send an inappropriate picture to a friend. Either way, the situation could escalate quickly, and you could find yourself in psychological, physical, and legal anguish. Step away, take a breath, and don't send it.

Remind yourself that your digital footprint allows anyone to see the person you are projecting yourself to be on social media. Parents of future significant others, future scholarship committees, future employers, and future neighbors will be able to look at your social media and make decisions about your character based on posts, pictures, shares, and comments that you have forgotten you published. When you engage in social media, you are publishing and representing your true character to the public. This content stays forever. So, what should you do when you are tempted to publish something out of emotion or anger or seduction or envy?

Step away. Take a breath. Don't send it.

Now, what if you have already done it? How do you walk through that fire? First, realize your life isn't over. At this point, you need to regroup and assess your emotional reaction. If you were coerced into sending pictures of yourself, many researchers are saying your response will be the same as if you were physically abused or sexually assaulted.[4] You will feel violated. You need to talk to a trusted adult. By working with someone such as your parents or a counselor at your school, you can move through the process to make sure you don't have lasting emotional scars from the event.

Sexting is another way young adults explore their sexuality and express their fun and flirty attitudes, but if you have received wounds from messages that became public or from messages you now regret sending, I encourage you to open up to someone you trust, so you can work through the problems. I'm sure other areas of your life are affected even if you don't necessarily connect the cause/effect. If you are having trouble sleeping, concentrating, or keeping an appetite, you might be experiencing physical effects of publishing inappropriate texts or posts.

Sending the emotionally charged text or post does not make you a bad person; humanity is full of all of us stumbling along, trying to make life better. If you have made this mistake and are feeling the guilt from your action, confide in someone you trust and move on to a new and better season of your life. If you are contemplating a post or message, just don't send it. Take a breath and realize you are better off without the verbal sparring and over-sharing.

—⁓—

Reflection

- What is your weakness with technology?
- How can you overcome this weakness?
- What has happened with technology in your past that might prompt you to discuss the emotional effects with someone you trust?

—⁓—

Your Space

You Cannot Marry Your High School Sweetheart

Dear Auspicious You,

I met my husband in the 4th grade, and my first secret crushes on him happened when we were in junior high. We tried dating a couple of times as underclassmen in high school, but it didn't work out. At Christmas of our senior year, we began to date again, and we haven't broken up since then. That was in 1985.

Before you start to cry "hypocrite" to describe me, listen. I believe you can't marry your high school sweetheart, and I also believe high school and college romances will not stand up to the pressures of marriage. If you are still in a relationship with your high school or college sweetheart, you must make the decision and the commitment to grow with each other and not fall apart while each individual becomes the adult version of him/herself. If you do grow apart, you should realize it's ok. Either way, you cannot remain the same person you were in high school.

A long time ago, I heard one of the wisest discussions about dating. We were camping and sitting around a fall campfire, which brings out better conversations than almost anywhere else in the world. My friend Brett explained dating to the crowd of junior high and high school kids gathered at the fire with us.[5] Brett pointed out that dating is a way to learn about the traits you need in a future mate. While you are in a high school or college romance, you are learning about the actions and words that make you feel loved as well as the actions and words that annoy you beyond belief. Brett suggested two people in a relationship can recognize their own shortcomings as well, and then both people can work to become better communicators and better partners as a couple.

He told the kids when they knew they were not going to marry a person they were dating, they should break up. Period. No one needs to wallow in a situation making you uncomfortable where you are not learning anything new about yourself. And, no one should ever cheat on a significant other because that action will destroy your own character and your partner's esteem. Later, when you are ready for a new significant other, you need to remember what you learned and look for someone with the traits fitting with your personality. You also need to remember what you learned about yourself and work to improve where your interpersonal relationship skills are weak. Isn't that good?

This advice helps you see young romance for exactly what it is meant to be, a training ground. You must practice honesty and sharing your life with someone else. You need to practice trust and knowing how much to lean on someone else as you balance growing as a couple with growing as individuals.

Can you handle someone who gets angry when you are assigned a group project in class because you are talking to other boys? What happens when your girl demands you sit with her at lunch and every sporting event which means you are missing out on the fun and fellowship with your friends? If you are wrapped up in young romance, you will accept these demands, at first. Then, you will most likely become resentful of someone else telling you what to do. Even then, I've watched as teen couples still try to stick together.

I don't understand at all because I know those same students are trying desperately to create their own identity separate from their parents and caregivers. They get angry when the adults in their lives tell them what to do but will begrudgingly accept such directives from a boyfriend or girlfriend. I would love for someone to explain this to me.

A romance when you are young is wonderful. The emotions run high, and the excitement is new and delicious! You are learning about another person and sharing your own story as well. Butterflies flutter incessantly in your belly! Yet, my auspicious one, that's not really love. Not yet. As the high emotions fade a little and you recognize some of the traits you need to improve, you both begin to change. The love happens when you grow together instead of apart.

My high school romance could have been a movie script. We both dated other people on and off but kept coming back to each other. It's like we instinctively knew we had more growing up to do before we were able to mature together as a couple. He was an integral member of the standout basketball team when we were seniors, and I was the captain of the cheer squad. Our families liked each other. My dad would boast about this high school version of my husband, and my mom and sisters approved. His family liked me, too.

Our last first date happened in December of 1985 when I was the decoy for his surprise birthday party our senior year. His parents planned the party, and I agreed to go on a "date" with him after a basketball game. I followed his mom's directions and insisted that we stop at his church to pick up some dishes for her. When we arrived, all our friends jumped out to surprise him. We started dating again that night and haven't broken up since.

In the spring of 1986, our senior prom was a fun time, and graduation had us looking at a bright future. Our parents agreed he could come on our family vacation to Kentucky Lake the summer after we graduated. All the families who camped with us enjoyed having him around, and my nieces and nephew loved him, too. Those first years were full of excitement and learning about ourselves and each other. Then, reality hit us hard as we went separate directions for college and as we each developed our own identity of who we were after high school. During this time, I learned a boyfriend and girlfriend must prioritize their own growth before any substantial foundation can support their loving each other as adults. It didn't matter that our high school romance seemed picture perfect. We were oceans away from being mature enough or prepared enough for an adult relationship that would stand as a solid marriage.

Looking back, I also realize a benefit we had. Even though our collective group of families and friends supported our dating, no one ever tried to make decisions for us in our relationship. Now, zoom out for a minute and look at your situation. How do the people around you and your boyfriend or girlfriend treat you as a couple? No adults or friends should ever pressure either partner into believing you will marry just because you are a couple in high school or college. My husband and I were blessed because we never felt this burden. Making your own choice without outside influence from well-meaning others is a key to your success with a high school romance becoming an adult love. The integrity of your choices is as important as becoming individual adults before becoming a husband and wife.

You and I have both known young adults who feel a little (or completely) trapped in a relationship because of expectations from other people. Sometimes when families get involved with a high school couple, they begin treating the couple as if they were already married. The freedom from this arrangement is enticing for the kids at first, but the couple doesn't understand they are handing away their power of choice.

The pressures that come with acting married too quickly end up creating a tangled mess. The families might begin hanging out together, creating memories, inside jokes, and traditions that sit squarely on the shoulders of the young couple. After this integration of family and friend circles, what will happen if the couple decides to go their separate ways? If the moms are now best friends who plan events together, will their relationship be wrecked if the girl breaks up with the boy? If a boy innocently begins to help his girl's grandparents because he genuinely enjoys being around them, how will they deal with not being able to depend on him to help with daily chores or visits after he breaks up and moves to college? If you are dating someone now, and your family and friends are getting too involved, I encourage you to sit down and have a conversation with them. You can openly talk about the pressure they are adding to your life by pushing you into a serious relationship, and together you can decide how they can show support for you and your significant other without adding the unnecessary expectations.

On the other hand, what if your family and inner circle do not support your choice of a significant other? Romeo and Juliet never had a chance for a happy ending because of their feuding families' disapproval of their relationship. When you are forbidden to have or do something, it's human nature to almost obsess over the banned object. The same goes for a banned relationship.

If this scenario represents your current relationship, you need to answer a few questions for yourself. Who is against this relationship? Why are they not in favor? Have you specifically talked to the person who doesn't approve? If your supporters don't like the new guy that you find interesting, you need to gather information before the relationship goes any farther.

You might not want to hear this again, but trusted people with an outside view do have experience and can see possible problems before they happen. You should talk to the ones who don't approve and ask for specific reasons. See if those reasons make logical sense. Can you refute the reasons with your own information?

If your parents or roommates or co-workers are concerned because the potential suitor has been in trouble with the police or has a huge amount of debt or tends to drink excessively, shouldn't you protect yourself and analyze the facts? Are these folks right? If you think the guy is cute and romantic and a little edgy, your emotions will be taking more control than your intelligence. If you truly believe the potential relationship could be a good one, you need to weigh the accurate evidence about how connecting yourself to this person will affect you. Do you share a similar vision for the future? Will you be able to grow in trust and support with this person? How will you help each other mature and serve?

If you answer these questions honestly, and with a good amount of solid evidence, you can see if this relationship is worth pursuing. Then, you can also talk to the ones who are against the connection to show that you've put forth a sincere effort in making this decision for yourself. As in all other situations, you must then be ready to take the benefits and consequences based on your choice to enter the relationship.

I do believe in romance, and in knowing at a young age when you are attracted to someone, but I will stand as a forever believer that you can't marry your high school sweetheart. By the time I walked down the aisle with my high school boyfriend, we had both changed from the teenagers we were at his surprise party. We weren't even the graduates who vacationed at the lake or the college kids trying to find our way in the adult world. Emotional romance comes and goes, but love matures. Love is a choice, and if you are going to marry the person you dated as a young adult, you both need to choose to grow and develop first as individuals and then as a couple.

—◦◦◦—

Reflection

- If you are dating someone right now, what signs show you are on solid ground to build a lasting relationship?
- Are either one of you jealous or demanding of attention? How does this trait surface?
- How do you handle being alone or hanging out separately with other friends?
- Does your boyfriend or girlfriend make decisions for you, or can you talk through a situation or decision and then ultimately choose to do what you feel is the best for you?
- Are either sets of families or friends subtly, or obviously, pressuring you to stay together or to break up? How?
- How do you want to grow as an individual and an adult? How does your goal complement your boyfriend or girlfriend?

—⁓—

Your Space

Who Do You Love?

Dear Auspicious You,

uickly! Don't think much, just answer these questions straight from your heart.

List the top three items you love about your favorite place in the world.

1.
2.
3.

List three ways your favorite animal makes you laugh.

1.
2.
3.

List three amazing traits of your best friend.

1.
2.
3.

List three reasons you love yourself.

1.
2.
3.

—∿∿—

Uh. Hmm. What happened with that last question? Why did you hesitate? Why can you rattle off nine different reasons to love a place, a pet, and a friend, but you had to pause and think about why you love you? I know questions about your own strengths make you crazy because it feels too much like bragging. Perhaps you haven't invested enough time contemplating why you are awesome. I guess it's also possible you don't love yourself, so the question is a stretch for you. If you're not sure how you feel about self-love, you might have a rough time with other relationships as well. How do you handle being alone? Do you like spending time with yourself?

When I was a kid, we had a pickup camper. My dad stored it in the backyard, and I spent hours and hours there by myself. I especially loved being in the camper when a summer storm rolled over our house because the sound of the rain on the roof and the thunder bubbling up all around me created the perfect setting for a cozy day. The little truck camper, propped up on the four-corner stabilizers, held my music, books, journals, and card games. The best naps of my nine-year-old life happened there. Since my sisters were older and out of the house, I learned to entertain myself, and the camper helped me realize how much I enjoyed my own company.

From hanging out in the camper, I started developing a value system I didn't even know I needed. I can look back and realize how spending time alone as a younger version of myself helped me prepare for those high-stakes moments later in life such as when I pulled away from the pressure of group-think in college. My afternoons in the camper taught me to believe in my own dreams and to spend quiet moments thinking about my relationships with my family.

As cliché as it sounds, successful adults have a true appreciation and love for themselves. Part of the journey and process of maturing is enjoying your own company and being able to do things by yourself. Before you get too far into college life, you will need to outgrow the "whole group to the bathroom" mentality and figure out how you see yourself. Even though it's difficult to think about when and how you lost your sense of self-love or self-esteem, we all need to sort through those times.

You have lived long enough to know the pain life can deliver. Disappointment, loss, trauma, abuse, sickness, and anxiety can all cause us to not like who we see in the mirror. I urge you to do the hard work of reflecting on your past to pinpoint any events that might cause you to dislike yourself or think that you aren't good enough. Just like any other relationship, self-love takes time and effort. You must be willing to identify what you see as the negative details about yourself. However, after you name the negativity, consider the source of it. Why do you consider this trait negative? Do other people plant doubts about your skill, appearance, or ability? You won't be able to wholly commit to a relationship if you are always trying to be someone else or meet the demands of another person. Be confident in your own identity. When you recognize that external situations have influenced your internal voice negatively, you can teach the internal voice a new language.

If the little conscience voice in your head always tears you down with harsh words, change the tone. If you don't do well on a test, your inner voice might say, "I'm such a loser." Instead, force yourself to say, "I didn't do well this time, but I will keep trying." Set small, measurable goals for yourself, and when you reach a goal, allow yourself to celebrate. Study for 20 minutes with your phone turned off and put in a drawer. When you allow yourself to stay focused and learn new material, you will be proud of yourself. Also, practice gratitude toward yourself. Find the parts of your personality for which you are grateful. Small steps will help you make huge strides toward a better self-outlook.

Personally, my negative self-talk started in early elementary school. I was unsure of myself, overweight, shy with classmates, and terribly homesick. I felt comfortable in a room of adults and could converse with ease, but kids my age scared me. I didn't know how to handle conflict, and I felt anxious when any discipline issues happened in class. I cried over leaving my mom. I don't have a clear idea of how many days I cried when she left me at school, but I'm certain the tears rolled almost every day.

Most of my issues stemmed from fear. The fear that my parents would die haunted me because I knew they were older than my friends' parents. This might seem irrational, but our family suffered many losses when I was too young to understand but old enough to remember the events. My maternal grandfather died before I was born, but I still felt the loss. My paternal grandmother died when I was four, and as a seven-year-old, I was at the house when my maternal grandmother suffered a heart attack and passed away. We also lost extended family members within a few months of each other. My cousins and I spent time at the funeral home on a regular basis and knew the best place to play Red Rover on the porch as well as how to make the perfect cup of lemonade from the packets in the back room.

The familiarity with the funeral home also spurred dreams where I would walk up to the casket expecting my dad to be in it. I wanted to cover him with my red, quilted blanket, but he wasn't there when I looked inside. I still vividly remember that dream, and it still makes me uneasy. No wonder I cried when I was away from my parents and had no idea how to express a confidence about myself.

These losses shaped my early childhood, and I didn't recover well. Yet, when I started spending time in the camper and enjoying being alone with myself, I changed. Even though I was too young to purposefully develop or recognize my new ability to be at ease on my own, the new skill proved to be a blessing. I started going to the town library by myself, and I could spend the whole afternoon exploring our creek, walking trails, and swinging on grapevines at our farm. Each of these activities that I experienced in solitude, alone with myself, created a space for my confidence to grow.

Does my story encourage you to investigate your own inner relationship? The most important relationship you can develop at this stage in your life is the one you have with yourself. When you are comfortable in your own skin, you will be confident and willing to meet the challenges ahead of you. You will also be willing to try new activities and enjoy the process of learning and growing.

As you establish yourself in the upperclassman role in high school and in the role of a college student, you will need to be a friend and an advocate for yourself. Already, you have so many excellent qualities! Look at the positive ways you influence the world and continue to advance the view you have of yourself. Stop being your own worst critic and recognize all the gifts and talents you have. Perfection isn't possible, so let go of that expectation. Take stock of your positive qualities and the activities you enjoy. You can learn to be alone without being lonely and to understand self-love as the most important relationship you can cultivate.

—⁓—

Reflection

- What are three reasons that you love yourself?
- How and when did you begin improving your relationship with yourself?
- What events have shaped your negative self-talk?
- After reading my letter what steps will you take to love yourself?

———

Your Space

PART TWO

Stress

How do you eat an elephant?

You probably can't go for even an hour in the morning without hearing someone complain they are stressed and freaking out over a test, a project, a decision, a new job, a relationship, or any other regular, everyday event. Living in a state of stress seems to be the norm, and every tough situation apparently causes a negative reaction. Instead of running for the squeezy stress balls when we are confronted by a big task, why can't we buckle down to work and enjoy the challenge?

How do you react to intense pressure? Do you have the reflex of fight or flight? You are a young adult who tries to juggle all your responsibilities, and I've noticed you allow yourself to take every well-meaning warning or scare-tactic as truth. You think tasks seem overwhelming all at once, and you have forgotten how to eat an elephant.

That's right. One bite at a time. Exactly like you are supposed to tackle all your pressing responsibilities. One step at a time. Very bright people on the edge of an exciting leap into a new adventure will freeze and question their own decisions and abilities. I want to make sure you are prepared and ready to fly. My letters to you in this section will sometimes deliver gentle encouragement and sometimes provide a swift kick in the pants to remind you to not fall prey to your own logical fallacies. For these letters, my focus is your logos, logic, and mind. You are bright, and I expect you to use your brain when stress knocks on your heart's door.

—◦∞◦—

Don't Play While You Work or Work While You Play

Dear Auspicious You,

Freshman year of college. Oh, the excitement and fear all rolled into one big ball of independence! Around first semester midterm of your first year of college, don't be surprised if the freshman panic mode begins in earnest. Some students are homesick, some are loving college/Greek life, and some are enjoying new freedoms, but it seems all students who care about their future goals become flustered about their grades. I'm sure you will be facing some rough classes and emotions, too, like every other beginning college student.

Many adults in your life try to tell you how college life will be and how much different it is than high school, but I know until you get there and experience it for yourself, you will never believe us. I have personally experienced a miserable stint of a freshman year and then have watched as thirty years of seniors moved to the next level of schooling. In each case, the freshman year offers challenges and obstacles for anyone attempting college.

It is the year where you don't have the support of parents at your beck and call, you aren't one of the oldest and best students at the school, and you have to re-image yourself. Your identity becomes a few degrees more in focus, and even though this year doesn't solidify who you are or who you want to become, the year forces you to decide how hard you are willing to fight for your dreams. Basically, it's rough all around.

You might end up with a couple of classes that leave you scratching your head about test grades, study habits, course preparation, or writing papers for "numbers" classes. Do you remember the first time you put in your full effort on a paper or project? If you are like my students and me, you worked for over an hour *planning* one draft of one paper. Then, you spent countless additional hours on the computer to nail down drafts of papers and other assignments.

All the learning from your work is not to be left at your previous school. The skills you were learning then should be the ones you apply to your studies now. The amount of focused time spent developing the quality of your thinking will certainly help you battle the newbie panic mode creeping up on you. You must decide if a professor wants you to do a critique or a comparative analysis…even in calculus or in biology…even with numbers instead of words.

Gone are the days when you will be able to memorize facts or listen and participate in class and then do well on the assessments. The skills of critical reading (having a conversation with an author), organizing thoughts by points of an argument, and incorporating your voice into the conversation with the other expert voices are skills applied to all areas. It's a whole new ballgame in college, but you already have experience with the basic skills.

Now, let's dig into how you are studying. When students truly focus on their studies, they have no phone, iPod, gaming system, social media, TV, or other distractions to interrupt the flow of work. Focused students don't talk about other issues. Are you removing the interferences when you study? It is honestly bull when people tell me that they study better with music playing or with the TV going or whatever else they might "need." Our brains simply don't work that way even if your headphones are noise cancelling.

You are a smart student who would enjoy the information, so do the research concerning the functioning of your brain.[6] I have been fascinated by what I've learned about our brains. We can give complete attention to only one stimulus at a time. If you are studying alone, get in a quiet spot away from all else. If you study with a group, great! But realize the distractions can be really tempting. If you are a very social person, and if a group study date includes food, an impromptu game of some sort, social media, and talk of current events, then it is NOT effective for learning (for socializing, yes, but learning, no). Your group must reel itself in before it will be effective for you. You might ask the other group members if they study alone as well as with the group. Ones with the exceptional grades will most likely say yes. I loved studying with my group in college; they had insights and could explain concepts in a way that really helped me. However, I had to study alone before AND after the group session to first prepare and then to solidify all we covered. Make it a priority to have the self-discipline to *prepare* to study because this will make or break you academically.

Also, our brain absorbs information in chunks. Think of the alphabet song...ab cd efg hi jk lmnop... Do you see all those letters squished together at the end? Little kids have trouble with this section of the alphabet because there are too many letters together. Think of phone numbers and social security numbers. These are in small chunks for us to remember them. How are you "chunking" your course material? Do you listen to lecture, hand write notes, go back after class and type those notes, color code them, and print them out to put in binder to add more hand notes at next lecture? Figure out how to chunk information for your brain instead of giving it too much to digest all at once.

What about the textbook reading? Josiah, a man who's now in medical school, shared with me how a professor pulled him aside and said he was doing great with the test questions covered in class discussion, but he was struggling with the questions over text material. First, let me point out a professor doesn't have to provide this level of personalization. I was impressed to learn how the teacher wrote and graded her own tests. Many lead professors of entry-level courses with a large number of students rely on teaching assistants and rarely see student work themselves. Also, it's amazing this teacher recognized a pattern with Josiah's tests and then took the time to talk to him about it. This professor saw the potential in Josiah, which, by the way, is cool because he was already standing out to the professors as a freshman! At that point, Josiah needed to act on the valuable information the professor gave him.

We conversed about how he was preparing for test questions from a book. I encouraged him to think back to high school study tips such as reading critically, annotating, note-taking, and using rhetorical analysis strategies. The other important strategies such as explaining what the text author is saying (as well as how he is saying it), discovering binaries, looking for repetition, learning vocabulary, and gaining background knowledge are also important tools to discover meaning within course readings. All these reading/thinking strategies would help him attack any texts, not just the ones from high school. The same principles apply to you. You need to be utilizing these strategies on each of your reading assignments, and yes, this type of preparation will take a lot of time. However, the benefit will be worth the effort.

And, speaking of professors, have you gone to see any of them during their office hours? This is a big change from high school. I'm pretty sure you are thinking like a high school kid still by thinking that going and asking for help is like brown-nosing or seeming weak. Not so. Going to office hours to prepare for a test or go over a reading or ask about a paper is mandatory. You are paying a hefty tuition for their expertise, and the professors will help those who help themselves.

Make an appointment and go to the offices. Ask your professors about the tutoring services because each campus will offer help in all subjects. Not only do you learn more, but the professors then recognize you as someone who cares and who is meeting the challenge of adulthood and taking care of the business at hand. The trip to a prof's office isn't about pride. You go because you are getting your money's worth and, most importantly, because *you must be an advocate for yourself.* No one is going to fight your battles for you, ever, in any situation, in any future. This is your first step into the adult world of figuring out what you need and then going to get it. This lesson will apply in every aspect of the years to come.

If you are feeling stress or anxiety, I also encourage you to decide if you are looking too far into the future all at once. Are you thinking and stressing about your grade point average for graduate school with every assignment and test even though grad school is years away? Maybe it's time to learn about you and how to be an adult and not stress about a future professional school. Remember to eat the elephant one spoonful at a time. Don't worry about graduate school right now.

Think about the next assignment or the next reading or the next test. Take the next step. Make excellent preparation your mantra. The rest will take care of itself. A graduate school might be your choice now, but you might choose something else later in your college life. Try not to put extra burdens on yourself. Take a break from self-imposed pressure and complete the next task; take the next step with your current responsibilities. You will find success when you plan and eat one spoonful at a time.

Hopefully, once you have experienced a few weeks of college life yourself, you will recognize my advice as solid and then act on it. Don't sell yourself short as you face the post-secondary world as an adult for the first time. How do you plan to handle the adversity? I'm sure if a younger student were to ask you about high school and difficult lessons to be learned in classes and on the extra-curricular fields and floors, you would know exactly what to say and how to help him. You faced high school adversity and mastered it.

This is no different because each step of your life builds experiences to help with the next one. Your senior year of college will also be stressful. Your future marriage (with a mortgage, kids, car payments, and life events) will be stressful. Your future career will be stressful. I can verify that the lessons I learned my freshman year of college were more about myself than any subject. Those lessons have shaped me and prepared me for marriage, infertility treatments/surgeries, home ownership, career choices, family illnesses, and raising children.

It will be the same for you. What you learn as a beginning college student will be mostly about you. How hard are you willing to fight? How many hours are you willing to spend? How much social/technology time are you willing to forfeit? It's all about choices because you are very smart and capable. You have talents waiting for you to develop them more fully. You have what it takes to be successful in college, and I am very proud of you. Growing up is hard and second-guessing is inevitable, but you can do this. However, you must remember the most important part: recognize where you need to step up your studying and then put in your serious effort. You will enjoy the breathing room you create for yourself, and you will enjoy the adult you create within yourself.

Reflection

- How can you improve your study habits?
- What kinds of assignments are the most difficult for you?
- What resources can you use to help yourself better prepare for classes?

Your Space

Take the Next Step

Dear Auspicious You,

Growing pains are awful. You know that, right? I'm certain you've felt the hurt of disappointment and wondered why your plans didn't work out as you intended. When your dreams fall short, the result of the failure is visible in your eyes, the set of your jaw, and the forward slump of your shoulders. You feel the distress associated with trying to come to grips with not getting what you have worked to achieve.

Depending on the failure, you are also questioning your ability to move forward. When you recognize how you didn't measure up to the expectations of the people who assisted in making your plan a reality, you must also face serious questions about your goals and abilities. Well-meaning adults say you can achieve any goal you put your mind to accomplishing. You've heard the platitude all your life. If you work hard, put in extra time, stay focused, ask questions, and commit to doing your best, then you will be successful with any dream you desire.

Except, sometimes this line is a lie.

Some of your goals won't work out even when you truly tried your best. What then?

Failures can be life-changing and painful. I've witnessed a student who dreamed his whole life of pursuing a certain career. Matt wanted to play college baseball and then move up the coaching ladder. This young man was talented and did have the potential to meet this goal with a full head of steam. Matt moved beyond the dream and spent two years preparing mentally and physically to meet stringent requirements for the field. He began the process to achieve his goal and found himself very successful through the beginning stages of recruitment. Then, because of an auto accident which was no fault of his own, an injury removed him from the course he planned. Matt's dream evaporated into x-rays and doctor's appointments, and he found himself physically hurt, mentally and spiritually empty, and at a loss for what to do next.

Other students have also felt the agony of lost dreams after they pursued each detail perfectly. I have been blessed to know students who are extremely smart, organized, and well-spoken. Every year my small, rural Indiana school has several students in the running for prestigious scholarships, and we help them prepare for the written essays and personal interviews as much as we can. These students spend hours tinkering with word choice and organization for their application materials, and they move through draft after draft to give the best representation of themselves. They practice answering possible interview questions and spend efforts familiarizing themselves with local and national news to have well-rounded knowledge as a base for the selection process.

Throughout the years, we've been able to congratulate several winners of their awards, but we also have had many who didn't get selected. This outcome does not reflect the potential or change the value of the students who didn't win a scholarship. When some of the students that I mentored didn't win, I couldn't provide any answers or help for improvement because they did perform each step to the best of their ability. If the whole "you can achieve any goal with hard work" rule were always true, these students would have won full ride scholarships instead of a thanks-for-applying email.

At the other end of the spectrum, though, with some situations hard work does pay dividends for your future. I can share the story of a student named Steve. He wasn't a star student because classroom work wasn't high on his priority list. This guy was amazing with mechanical workings of engines, and he expanded his knowledge in the field. By the time he was a senior, he was highly skilled. If a vehicle had a motor, he could take it apart, put it back together, repair it, and maintain it. He was the guy you wanted to take care of your car. However, he was at risk to not graduate because he hated English.

He didn't see the value in reading and writing because those tasks didn't have a direct impact on what he did in a garage. He would put in half-hearted efforts with coursework, and many times, he didn't turn in assignments at all. He thought the teacher hated him. He was dejected and upset that his efforts in class still resulted in poor marks. The low scores and the missing work caused him to face the possibility of having to make up the credit for first semester.

I found Steve in the guidance office one late fall afternoon as he was preparing to drop out of high school. He'd had all he could take. After our long and serious conversation, he promised to think about his decision over the weekend. He talked to his support system at home and made the choice that changed his life.

From that point on, Steve committed to earning a diploma. We worked on assignments for his class together, and although he continued to have setbacks, he did put in serious effort and earned his diploma. During that year, he learned the difference between an adult's effort and a teenage boy's attempt to focus and complete a difficult task. Early in the year, Steve wanted to blame his lack of success on the teacher, on the "stupid" subject, and on the apparent irrelevancy of the material. When he figured out what focused work felt like and looked like, a new door opened for him.

After graduation, Steve enrolled in a technical college. The work was not easy for him, but he used his newly developed skills for his written coursework. In the mechanical work, he continued to be a rock star. He earned his next degree on schedule, and he now holds an awesome job that allows him to travel with a racing company and supports his own competitive racing as well.

Learning to deal with disappointment without losing your drive is imperative for you to be successful in life. As a young teacher, I applied for jobs I didn't get which meant I had to work through the disappointment as I continued a job search. A few weeks ago, I turned in syllabi just to have my work rejected, so I had to return to the process and revise my plans again. More than once, I created a new dish for dinner, but ended up throwing it out because of my Pinterest fail, and I still cooked again the next day to feed my family.

I'm not sure which of these types of failures describe you. I am, however, sure that you have failed in some way. If you haven't failed by now, then you aren't chasing a big enough dream. Are you like Matt who worked for years to prepare for a goal that was snatched from him? Maybe like Steve, you thought you were putting in more effort than you did, which caused a failure.

Losing a dream can range from an annoying inconvenience to a devastating toll on you mentally and physically. Where did you fail? To truly rebound from the situation, you need to recognize and name the specific goal you had. What did you want? Why? Try to gain perspective in the midst of pain.

Instead of blaming others, step away from yourself and search your emotions. What can you do differently to achieve a different outcome? For some reason, students think they need to be strong and face the trials alone. They don't want to show any weakness. Because of this false exterior, some students even refuse to talk to teachers or professors to accept help from experts. How can you make connections with adults who can offer encouragement? Who would that be?

Another pitfall of failure happens when you compare yourself to others because misplaced comparisons help no one. Young adults seem to constantly compare themselves to peers, and to be healthy, the practice must stop. Comparisons can lead to feelings of jealousy, inadequacy, anger, and frustration. If you have failed to reach a goal, but one of your friends succeeds, you will wonder what's wrong with you.

True maturity will allow you to notice and validate other people without sliding into the problem of comparing yourself to someone else. I know the level of difficulty that I'm proposing because our culture is based so heavily on competitive beliefs and behaviors. I'm all for good competition, but I don't want you to let the messages around you impact your ability to be happy for others while you are chasing your own dreams.

Give compliments! When you see one of your friends doing well, tell him. An earned scholarship, a new job, or a good grade in a difficult course offer perfect opportunities for you to acknowledge the work and dedication your friend has put forth. When you allow yourself to be genuinely happy for someone else, without being jealous, you will grow stronger. If you find your brain drawing a T-Chart comparing you to someone else, ask yourself why.[7]

Other people make their lives look like such a success on social media, so no good will come from comparing your reality to their lens-filtered life. When you are trying to decide which major is best for you or which clothes to wear or which campus job to pursue, don't look at others. Even if you fail along the way, you must determine your own purpose and be diligent with following the best path to achieving it. Allow your inner circle to support you through discussions and honest questions, but don't second-guess every goal because of misplaced comparisons with peripheral friends. One of the most damaging ways that you can fail yourself is permitting yourself to compare your life to other lives.

As you search your heart concerning your failure, remember all experiences lead to new knowledge about yourself and the world around you. It's important for you to see the failure as a loss, so you can more effectively adjust to how you want to proceed. You will have to work through the emotional aspects of the loss before you are ready to logically think through what happened.

The most important idea I want to impress on you is to recognize the action as a failure, but not yourself. You are not a failure. The unachieved object might have been out of your control, or a set of processes you were using to achieve a goal did not work. Even though you have experienced a setback when things didn't go according to your plan, you should never quit *growing*. You have different opportunities and options to pursue as you adjust and review and revise your goal. As you work through the emotional and mental steps and refocus for a new goal, be encouraged by those of us who've also stepped through failure. Take the next step. You've got this.

———

Reflection

- Did you fail by losing something of value or by not accomplishing a goal?
- How did you prepare to achieve this goal?
- What can you do differently to have a different outcome?
- Do you still have the same goal? Why/Why not?

———

Your Space

Healthy Ways to Vent and Destroy Your Mason Jars

Dear Auspicious You,

Annie Dillard wrote a memoir about growing up in Pittsburgh titled *American Childhood*.[8] One of the most gripping moments in her stories happened when she was in elementary school and her class witnessed the opening of a Polyphemus moth from its cocoon. Her teacher placed the cocoon and the stick from which it hung in a mason jar, and when the moth began to emerge from the cocoon, all the students crowded around the desk to watch.

I can imagine that the classroom was in awe since this beautiful creature decided to emerge while they were in school and could witness the event. The students knew the Polyphemus moth boasts a wing-span of four to six inches and discussed the process it would follow. Once the moth freed itself from the cocoon, it would shake out the beautiful wings. When the blood filled the wings, they would harden like perfect sails. However, the emerging moth found itself at a life-threatening disadvantage as those unsuspecting elementary students stood and watched.

The mason jar was too small. The poor moth climbed from the cocoon and shook its wings but was unable to reach the full six-inch wingspan. Instead, the wings hardened in an awkward bent shape, destined to never fly. The teacher marched the students outside where she shook the moth from the jar, and they all watched it walk up the street toward the housing district where students from the school eventually settled down after they grew into adults. Dillard writes that she was sure the moth would be smashed by a car or eaten by a cat before the afternoon was over. Isn't this memory awful for her?

My students react strongly to this story, and I use their response as a catalyst for a semester-long project. We discuss the mason jar of the story and turn it into a metaphor for any item, person, or situation that holds us back from reaching our potential. Sometimes, education itself is a mason jar. We've discussed how standardized testing, required courses, tuition costs, and hoop-jumping all become mason jars forcing students to suffer from awkwardly bent wings instead of flying full force into their futures. We also explore how some people become forces that impede progress when we give away too much power to someone else.

After the reading and discussion, each of my students receives a mason jar. Throughout the semester students write on slips of paper, recording what keeps them from being the best they can be. No one is allowed to look inside of a jar except for the owner, so the privacy and safety make the jars a healthy place for students to vent.

You can tell when students are having a rough day because they stomp in the room and head straight for their mason jar. I've witnessed some very forceful and angry openings of the jars with paper slammed into them. Sometimes, salty tears drop into the jar with their slip of paper. Comic relief happens, too, when my name shows up in everyone's jar at least once, usually around the time a major paper is due. The exercise is more than making a collection of hindrances, though. We make sure to provide ourselves with a much happier ending than Dillard's.

On the last day of class, like Dillard's teacher, I take my students outside as each person carries his mason jar. Then, we have some fun. First, each student burns the papers inside of his jar. After all the papers are nothing but ashes, the students get an opportunity to take a sledge hammer to their jars. That's right. We bust the jars into pieces, and it's awesome! The metaphor of burden and difficulty that we built all semester ends up a metaphor of breaking out and freedom. Each year, I'm prepared to begin a new class exercise, but my students want to do this one. Even after years pass, students talk to me about the mason jars and how much the process meant to them.

How many slips of paper would you have in your mason jar? I know as a young adult, you feel plenty of pressures keep you from reaching your full potential. Frustrations abound, and you must learn effective ways to deal with them. I can tell you from experience running away from frustrations, emotionally eating chocolate to solve problems, and spouting off mouthy comebacks don't provide effective tension-relieving tactics. You can find better ways.

Can you pinpoint the cause of your frustration? I mean the true cause, not the last event or person who happened to be too close when you finally came to the end of your rope. What causes you to feel overwhelmed? If you are like me, you will find when many tasks are due all at the same time and when you feel unable to process all the information and requests coming at you, the frustration gets worse.

You are in the season of your life right now where you probably have more major life events happening all at once than ever before. You are trying to manage the daily work and requirements of your time while you are also looking to the future and making big decisions that will affect you long-term. This kind of pressure is enough to push all of us into a bit of beast mode.

The trick is making sure that your beast mode doesn't make you a two-headed monster. If one of your friends happens to spill coffee on your new jacket, you don't need to respond in a fury. Accidents happen. When you do overreact, try taking a step back to find the real cause of your emotional response. Why such anger? Why the tears? Once you figure out the true trigger of your reaction, then you can talk to your friend and share how you are feeling.

I completely understand that you'd rather write down your feelings on a slip of paper and slide it into a mason jar instead of facing the problems aloud and walking deeper into your emotions, especially with someone else. Still, you will find that sharing the roots of your frustrations allows you to see the size and shape of what's causing you to be on edge. Talking about how big or small the issues feel makes them manageable, and venting these frustrations will help even if the problem doesn't magically go away.

Many small, daily obstructions can cause you big trouble and can push you to snap at the people closest to you. If this is happening, remind yourself of how to eat an elephant. Once you slow down, prioritize, take a breath, and then do the next thing, you will feel much better. You will then be able to manage the tasks, requests, assignments, jobs, and adult responsibilities coming your way.

What about the bigger problems, though?

If you are suffering from a more serious situation, simply taking a breath and creating a list of tasks to complete probably won't do much good. I didn't believe this until I felt it myself. I was the person who solved problems for others. I was good as a peacemaker, a planner and organizer, an action-taker. When someone mentioned how they felt depressed or anxious, I would think of several ways for the person to snap out of the problem and the emotion. Just take the next step, right? It's simply a matter of putting your mind to it and showing effort, right?

Not really.

Life's trials settled on me, and I was faced with the scenarios that frightened me the most. My mom's breast cancer metastasized into her liver. She passed away when I was a young wife and mother of 7-year-old twins. Even though I am squeamish beyond belief and I pass out when other people give blood, I was in the middle of providing the physical health care for my mother at the end of her life. I could turn on the organizer mode and manage all aspects of responsibilities around me without having to process any emotions.

Then, the night of my mom's viewing, my dad was taken out of the funeral home in an ambulance. That's when we found out he had lung cancer. We had to leave the funeral home after the visitation and go to the hospital with Dad. He was released to go to Mom's funeral the next morning. Because of the enormous weight of stress, I became a reservoir, letting nothing in or out.

After three years of ups and downs, my dad's cancer was impacting him more and more. I was still a young wife and mother, fighting with all my strength to not face this emotional roller coaster. Until I couldn't fight any longer.

I ended up with my husband, my doctor, my pastor, my friends, and my family supporting me as I could not get out of bed. I couldn't open the curtains in my room, leave the house without an anxiety attack, or eat. I don't know who fed my children or who helped them with their homework. I couldn't get in a car and drive to school. In those very dark days, I realized the truth about pushing emotions so far down inside of my chest that they packed my system full of a stagnant heaviness. As my body lost the ability to physically function normally, my mental ability to overcome the fear inside of me also dwindled. I was left with only myself, wondering who I was and what had happened to the strong me.

During this time my friends and family kept a close eye on me. My husband took control of the outside stimuli by sheltering me from unnecessary stress. My sisters called and chatted and helped me maintain a sense of normalcy. When I was able to return to work, my friends literally followed me around school, making sure I was still upright, eating, and driving safely. Slowly, I emerged on the other side of depression quite shell-shocked. I had no idea a person's ability to simply decide to quit being depressed didn't exist.

I put in the tough, emotional work of looking inside myself and sorting through the vulnerability and fear I had felt since I was the little kid playing with my cousins at the funeral home all those years before. I faced mortality in real-time, not in a far away memory or in a platitude.

My dad passed away a few weeks after I emerged from this darkness, and everyone around me was worried about how I would respond. I also wondered if I would retreat behind the closed curtains of my bedroom, and honestly, some moments I did. But, not for the same reasons.

I learned to talk with my trusted inner circle of people instead of pushing my emotions away, and I allowed myself to rest. I learned to recognize the signs in my own behavior when I needed to be alone to process information and emotions. I learned to see the beauty and the love around me through my family members as we continued to share our lives, holidays, vacations, and memories. These experiences allowed me to be more compassionate and understanding when real and tangible effects happened to me and to other people around me. I'm still a bit amazed I can write this letter to you as someone who's come through this fire.

If you are in the throes of a crisis, tell someone. My biggest mistakes happened because I tried to deal with every detail of life except for my own fears and emotions. And, I tried to do it all by myself. I would not consider admitting I needed someone to help me because my mind and heart were a mess.

While I did not feel a desire to inflict harm on myself, my sisters and doctor were quick to ask me if I did. I know from my experiences of helping students that self-harm is a dangerous path to take. If you feel yourself drawn to cutting, numbing your feelings with alcohol or drugs, thoughts of suicide, or any other forms of self-injury, talk to someone.[9]

Please hear me.

If you are feeling overwhelmed with the big problems of life and if depression and anxiety are taking root in your heart and soul, tell someone. Share your feelings with your parents. Have a friend go with you to your school's counselor. Tell a doctor at your school's clinic. You have many options to reach out to caring adults who will support you so that you do not have to walk through this season of life alone. Actually, you probably can't walk through it alone. Healing and health will return when you ask for help and then allow others to support you.

Whether your mason jars in life are small or life-changing events, you need to honor yourself enough to recognize them. Give your mason jars a name to understand the problems that hold you back from being a peaceful and productive you. Then, talk to someone. You will be amazed at the people who are just like you, struggling with their own mason jars. Even people who seem to have life figured out and seem to be doing much better than you are facing their own messes.

I promise.

Once you share your story, you will empower yourself to be healthier while you empower others to bravely break open their own jars.

—◦◦◦◦—

National Suicide Prevention Lifeline: 1-800-273-8255
http://suicidepreventionlifeline.org/

—◁◁◁◁▷—

Reflection

- What would you put in your mason jar?
- How can you train yourself to notice the small issues and deal with them before they become bigger problems?
- What actions do you take when you are feeling frustrated?
- Who can you talk to concerning your struggles?
- When have you felt overwhelmed in a more serious way?
- To what extent have you felt real depression? How do you deal with it?

—◁◁◁◁▷—

Your Space

Homesick, Lost, and Lonely

Dear Auspicious You,

How are you doing? Do you find yourself staying on top of your grades and assignments, or are you slipping a little? Do you find your mind wandering to another time and place? Does this daydreaming distract you? Maybe you are having a bit more trouble than a little daydreaming. Are you able to concentrate, or do you have a pit in the bottom of your stomach reminding you that your childhood, easier days, and maybe even your family are farther away than ever? How are you handling being more on your own than any previous time?

Perhaps some of the problem with high school senioritis and with succeeding as a new college student deals with being homesick. These two might not seem related at first, but students are homesick for many different people and seasons of life. Whether your homesickness comes from missing a lost childhood, a lost pet, a lost person, or a lost place, most people can relate to your situation. Personally, I had a difficult first year of college because I was extremely homesick.

As I have already shared with you, my high school years passed quickly and provided me with wonderful relationships and lessons. During those formative years, I felt supported, challenged, loved, and satisfied. I loved high school so much that the experience reinforced my calling to work with young people, and I geared my professional career around making a difference for other high school students by becoming a teacher. I was excited to move into my college dorm room with expectations of even better experiences than high school brought me. On the day I moved into the dorm, the bright sunshine welcomed me to campus. We hauled all my belongings up to the thirteenth floor of Blumberg Hall at Indiana State University. My roommate was a close, life-long friend named Maria, and we had plans for this new journey.

Our parents settled us into the room and then headed home, which was only a little over an hour away. We made it to college, freedom, and adventure! The first days of classes passed with introductions, syllabus adjustments, materials and books, exploring campus, and cafeteria adventures. My high school sweetheart was in college at a different school a little over an hour away, and his adjustment was going well, too. Maria and I had fun preparing our room, and like any girl who loves organizing, I established my routine to have a smooth start to the year. I enjoyed the classes and professors, and I found the material wasn't overwhelming when I stayed true to my plans.

Then, a switch flipped. I'm not sure if it happened in my heart or my brain or a combination of the two, but suddenly I felt overwhelmed. I couldn't eat and started to lose weight. I found myself in tears for no apparent reason. I would call home and hear my family chatting in the background, knowing my sisters and their kids were all hanging out at our parents' house. I thought I was missing out on all their fun. A pit of dread took up permanent residence in my stomach, and suddenly, my confidence left me.

Before my first collegiate mid-term exam, my parents arrived in town to take Maria and me out to eat. I'm sure I looked miserable because I was desperate to go home, and

I was worried about the first test the next day. When we arrived back at the dorm, Maria went inside, but I stayed in the truck with my parents. I tearfully begged them to let me come home just for the night to study. I thought I'd prepare better at home.

My dad said no. He made me get out of the truck and walk back into the dorm. I found out later that he had to pull over several times on the way home because he was crying so much, wondering if he made the right decision. Years later, I was able to tell him that if he let me come home that night, I might have never gone back. His strength and willingness to push me ushered me to the next step of my maturing journey.

After I returned to my dorm, I dried my tears and studied. I realized I didn't have a choice, so I settled down, opened my books, and lost myself in the work. This method proved effective for me because when I studied, I wasn't sad. I ended up making good grades in part because I found my coping mechanism in learning.

I can't report the homesickness ended there. I came home every weekend, and I dreaded Sunday nights when I had to go back. I was miserable for quite a long time, but with each passing week, I learned to adjust and relax more. I'm still not sure why my transition to college was so difficult, but I learned about myself during this time.

When does your stomach drop and hurt because of homesickness? Do you miss being younger? Maybe you miss a time when life was simpler or before a life-changing event like a parents' divorce or a remarriage or a death? Does your homesickness affect your performance in school or your ability to fit in with a group of people or your decision-making skills?

When she was a college freshman, one of my past graduates, Tessa, wrote to me asking for advice about changing colleges and changing majors. Even though she had a very generous scholarship, she still felt unhappy and lonely at college. She wasn't sure what she wanted to study. Some of her high school friends advised her to transfer to their university, which was twenty minutes away from home. Did selecting a university and a course of study go smoothly for you? Have you faced the question about moving schools or changing your major because you are lonely and homesick?

If your longing for home makes you question your choice of university, you need to think through a few items. If you have a scholarship, will it follow you to any school? If not, stay put and give yourself a chance to settle into the new environment before you make any major changes. Attend a campus church group or a local church around campus. Join a club or an intramural sports team. Go to the gym on campus and sign up for yoga or cycling class. Force yourself to audition for a part in a play or work as a stagehand. Sign up to volunteer on a regular basis in an area of interest and then do it. Get a part-time job. Create opportunities for yourself to be in a community of people and then be in it.

Growing pains are very, very hard but also important. Are you really allowing yourself to adjust to college life, or are you staying in your room and going to class and shielding yourself from interacting with others? What community group have you consistently joined and participated in on a regular basis to give you a place to meet and learn about others? My freshman year was miserable, and only when I forced myself to become involved with others and volunteering did I feel lasting relief from my homesickness.

Face this step of growing up because the lessons you learn will last a lifetime. After I overcame the first-year hurdle, I was more prepared for when I felt it again. During my first year of teaching, I questioned myself and felt terribly unprepared, so the dread returned. Then, I was homesick for college, if you can believe that. I longed for the comfort of confidence in myself. Since I had overcome the problem once before, I was able to recognize my fear, call it out, and move forward. I found the homesickness and dread were all based in fear of the unknown that rendered me useless when I let it. Learning to overcome the mental battle was probably the single most important lesson I learned in college.

Furthermore, if you are feeling unsettled and wonder about the wisdom of making a change, recognize that choosing a different campus will not alleviate all your fear and being upset. Yes, you might end up back on the same campus with life-long friends and tons of other graduates from home, but it won't be the same as being in high school. You shouldn't want the college experience to be the same.

You can't grow and stretch yourself into the adult you have the potential to be when you hang on to the high school friendships and mentality. Even your solid and life-long friendships need to evolve and become more adult. You will still have to face challenges by yourself, deal with being alone, and set and chase your own dreams. On any campus, you will need to face the homesick feeling and press forward to meet new people, form new friendships, and stand on your own two feet. If you want to develop your gifts and talents, you must be open to expanding your network and circle of influence no matter which campus you attend. My mom used to quote an old Girl Scouts song lyric, "Make new friends, but keep the old. One is silver, and the other's gold."[10] She was right.

Now, about selecting the best place to pursue your major. Which campus boasts the best quality of education for you? Talk to students in your major to find out the level of dedication the campus and professors provide to keep instruction on the cutting edge for your field. Check out the job placement statistics and the grad school entrants. You might be more confident looking at data instead of feelings and emotions. Does one stand out more than the other?

You are bright enough to know both places have positive and negative aspects. That won't change. No matter which campus you're on, you will have good days and bad days, effective professors and awful ones. It might be time to remind you that happiness, as an emotion, is fleeting, fickle. True joy comes from a peace inside of you that shows maturity. Recognizing you will be both happy and sad at every location you'll ever encounter at every stage of your life should take off some of the pressure you are feeling. You simply can't find lasting happiness because life doesn't work that way. You can, however, experience true joy when you are peaceful even through rough circumstances.

You can't screw this up.

Any accredited school will offer you a piece of paper at the end, and this diploma will allow you to join the workforce and make a difference in people's lives while earning a good living. Worst case scenario is you take longer than you planned to finish because you change your mind more than once. Eventually, you will still end up with the coveted piece of paper allowing you to help others and support yourself. And in the meantime, you will be learning many lessons about life, yourself, and others, and those specific lessons will turn into new avenues for you to connect with and help people.

Lay down your need for perfection. Even brilliant students must learn how, unfortunately, social maturity isn't as easy to develop as book smarts. You can't just put your mind to it and memorize facts. You need to walk life's path and grow up as you face new situations. It's frightening and intimidating for everyone. Consider where you would most like to be and what you are most passionate about studying when you are both miserable and content while you move through these growing pains.

Just as I told Tessa, I'll tell you, too. The decision IS yours. As it needs to be. She decided to switch to the university closer to home and felt an instant relief with her choice. I think that's the key, a peaceful heart. Finding the relief of peace in your mind and soul allows you to feel positive about the decision you made for yourself. Still, you aren't alone in the decision because you can listen to advice and learn from others.

In the middle of all this maturing and growing, you need to quiet your soul and look inside to determine where you will find the most peace. Go read "The Road Not Taken" by Robert Frost.[11] Breathe. Remember that everyone is sad they can't travel both roads, but the path you do take will be ok. It will make a difference for you, and you will be glad for the opportunity.

I have faith in you, and I am always in your corner.

—◈◈◈—

Reflection

- What causes you to feel homesick?
- What have you done to alleviate feeling lonely?
- Why do you believe changing your major or your school will help you to be more settled?
- How much do you believe me that you will be both satisfied and lonely in every location you will be for the rest of your life? What does this claim make you realize?
- How do you plan to turn self-concerned homesickness into other-centered action?

—◈◈◈—

Your Space

Good Decisions for
Thursday Night

Dear Auspicious You,

Budweiser commercials are awesome. The Clydesdale horses tell the perfect story and those huge beasts are funny, helpful, empathetic, patriotic, and so beautiful. The Corona commercials paint the perfect beach scenario, and who doesn't love a perfect beach? Someday, maybe we can all be as suave as the Dos Equis guy. As a connoisseur of commercials, I am intrigued by the alcohol industry and the creativity the companies utilize to sell their products. The characters, plots, serial stories, pitch, and culture connections these commercials create lean toward pure genius at times, and I wouldn't mind running to the local package store to buy my own bottle of paradise and coolness.

Except for one small problem. I don't drink.

You might be surprised to learn I'm a bit of a control freak. Crazy, I know. But, it's true. I feel the need to be in control of me and the situations in which I place myself. As a young high school student, I realized that alcohol erased inhibitions, which frightened me to the point where I never wanted to act differently because of drinking. Plus, I absolutely hate the taste. No one has ever talked me into enjoying any type of alcohol I've tried. Not even my best girlfriends. Because I can't tolerate the taste and the loss of control so much, I have never been drunk.

I realize everyone has their vices, and drinking, smoking, and promiscuity top the charts as the most common actions leading many people to misfortune. I want to be honest with you and share that I haven't had trouble with these issues. Classmates who knew me well in high school and college would report that I was a "good girl" who loved to have fun but would draw very deep lines in the sand concerning certain behaviors. Basically, I was a such a "good girl" because of fear, which in hindsight, is fine by me.

However, I also want you to understand my compassion for people who do enjoy a smoke or who choose to attend parties where the hosts serve more than sweet tea. Judgment isn't on my agenda. My desire is for real conversations and helping folks find balance and moderation in their lives.

Unlike the other subjects we discuss, my personal background with these issues is based on life events of people close to me, and those stories aren't mine to tell. Still, I know for certain how your life is impacted by the opportunities to choose an evening of freedom aided by a little liquid encouragement. A young adult's life, as we both know, is full of temptations. Whether you are on a high school or a college campus, the opportunity to make poor choices comes up every day, and many of the young adults who decide to participate in this culture have talked to me as a trusted adult. Spurred on by this connection, I feel the conviction to write to you about the problems of excess.

Now that you know a little more of my background, let's see where you fit.

Many young adults participate in certain behaviors because of curiosity or pressure to fit in with a group. Young adults today are educated on the problems of peer pressure and curiosity; however, the pull toward harmful behaviors is still present. Before we go further, let me say first that you don't have to engage in risky activities to fit in with a group or to cope with stressors. If you look around, you will find others who don't participate in these behaviors, either. You can find other avenues away from the harmful ones.

Still, you see the culture on every type of media as well as in your own friends and families. Tobacco use, social drinking, sexual exploration, and sometimes social drug use infiltrates almost every avenue of your lives. The important question, however, focuses on how much you are willing to compromise or sacrifice to find your answer to the question of curiosity. In many cases a young adult can experiment with tobacco, alcohol, drugs, and sex without long-lasting effects, but the chance you will be facing long-term consequences does exist. Students have talked to me about both benign and painful situations, and the difference seems to be in the purpose of use.

If a young adult decides to go to a party where illegal activities are happening, their values system either guides them or disappears. The time to decide on your core values is not as you enter the door of the party or move to the back seat of a car. Your decisions about integrity and purpose must be solidified before you are in the actual situation; otherwise, you will act based on emotion or peer pressure. Still, even when you know where your limits are, you will find yourself in a place of exploration. At that point you should consider your motives.

One of my past students, Linda, confided that because of a parent's past trouble with drug addiction which landed the parent in jail, she vowed to herself she would never take even one unauthorized prescription pill or one hit of marijuana.

This promise to herself was sacred, and Linda understood all too intimately the troubles for a family when one of its members succumbed to the curiosity of drugs that eventually turned into more casual use and then addiction. She would not follow her parent down this path.

However, she did allow herself to explore the curiosity about tobacco. Linda learned the nicotine in vaping helped to calm her nerves and helped her to face the pressures of difficult classes, sports, college decisions, and family issues. Before she expected, she was addicted to the nicotine. When she was caught vaping on her high school campus, she faced the consequences, from both the school and the local authorities, of having tobacco on a tobacco-free campus as well as being underage and in possession of it.

When Linda and I talked about her punishment and her plan to move forward, she adamantly professed she could not quit the vaping. The addiction was too strong for her, and she thought it was impossible to stop, looking at the issue as a flaw in herself. I tried to point out that "impossible" was the wrong word for this situation.

She used vaping to deal with the pain and stress of other areas in her life, but this use didn't make her a bad person. She chose to continue using the tobacco to cope with the other parts of her life that made her feel poorly. When she felt more settled with grades, future decisions, and family, then she could choose to quit the vaping and tackle the awful symptoms of physical and emotional withdrawal from the tobacco.[12]

She wasn't a bad person, but in her situation, she was choosing to manage one set of bad feelings over another. Granted, the best scenario here would have been for her to talk to someone about the problems causing the stress in the first place, but that's not how real life works sometimes. She realized she could have dealt with her stress in a different way, but once she was in the situation, she needed to see the big picture to help her quit smoking.

Can you relate?

Maybe alcohol is your go-to as a stress reliever. Do you see how the same issues with Linda and her vaping can be applied to your alcohol use? Does it help you to relax and forget about your life stressors for a while? Maybe alcohol allows you to feel a freedom from the world and the pressures of never feeling good enough. For many people, casual drinking is not a problem. They can have a drink with dinner and move on without ever feeling overwhelmed.

But, what happens when you *need* a drink? One of my friends drinks quite often. Once, I heard him say he needed a drink, so he wasn't going to have one. I didn't understand, but his explanation made sense. He drinks because he wants to, not because he *has* to drink. If he ever feels like he needs a drink to take the edge off a stressful day, he will not let himself have the drink. Is this a clever way to mask alcoholism? I'm still not sure, but I do get the point. My concern for you in this situation is knowing yourself so well that you can monitor your own motivation concerning alcohol consumption.[13]

If you do, why do you drink? Do you drink every day? Do you need the drink? Have you allowed yourself to go overboard and become intoxicated to the point of sickness, memory loss, or blacking out? Why? Is this type of binge drinking a regular occurrence for you?

The party culture is alive and well on all high school and college campuses. All of them. How do you handle the freedom? For many college campuses, Thursday is the major party night because of students going other places over the weekend. How will you handle the decisions for your next Thursday night?

The inhibitions after alcohol use is one of the most frightening aspects to me. The news offers story after story of young men and women who are alone, drunk, and vulnerable in the middle of the night, trying to get back to their apartments. Some of them make it home safely, and some are lost forever. Literally lost. Never to be heard from again. Terrifying. Even when you make promises with your friends to stick together, the alcohol seems to make those promises fuzzy. Suddenly, you will find yourself separated from the others because the dance floor is packed with too many bodies, and when your group members aren't thinking clearly either, you can be left there alone. What then?

Reality can also play out differently with this scenario as well. Maybe you won't be literally lost, but what if you all aren't using logic, and you decide to leave with someone other than your group, and your group lets you go? Other than the horrific risks of abduction, rape, and murder after this scenario, a more subtle and excessively more likely outcome would be when you leave with someone and find yourself in an unfamiliar place and in unexpected arms when you come back to your senses.

Sexual choices are personal. No one can say yes to any amount of physical intimacy on your behalf. You must say yes for yourself. Unfortunately, alcohol, or even a room full of people and music and dancing, can impact your thoughts and choices. Suddenly, you will find yourself more open to and accepting of many physical encounters that you would normally turn down. People talk about the walk of shame almost like it is a badge of honor. It isn't.

Promiscuity can make you feel worthless and used, and this feeling can impact the way you see yourself in the future. When you are alone and thinking clearly, examine yourself. Why do you allow yourself to end up in precarious situations? You might act confused and uncertain about your motivation aloud and around others, but I am certain inside of your heart, you understand the reality of your seeking physical attention from others. You might even be able to pinpoint the reason sexual attention pleases you.

Your decisions concerning your body need to be your choices, and I encourage you to back off from this sort of attention when you begin feeling unsettled about the activity. Do some soul searching and discover the appeal. Why do you want to place yourself in this scene?

Did you know that people can have symptoms of post-traumatic stress disorder (PTSD) from any traumatic event? We normally associate a prognosis with military veterans, but young children who experience the trauma of losing a parent or teens who endure a controlling or abusive relationship can also suffer from the disease of PTSD.[14] Once you are hurt that deeply, you can have flashbacks, anxiety, and panic attacks triggered by various stimuli. The effects of PTSD might be the catalyst for engaging in harmful behavior. Are you struggling to push down the memories of your past and struggling to move forward?

While an event like this possibly explains your experiences with memory-affecting substances, you shouldn't try to handle an issue this serious by yourself. Tell your parents. Make an appointment with your school's counseling department or your doctor and talk through your past events and present struggles to create a plan and to learn various coping skills. Simply put, you might be able to stop making harmful choices when they are based on curiosity; however, if a more serious, inner wound prompts your reckless behavior, you deserve the help from a professional. You will feel so much better when you aren't struggling alone.

—⁓—

Alcohol
- Phone numbers to your local AA organizations on the website.
- https://www.aa.org/pages/en_US/index

Crisis Text Line
- Text HOME to 741741
- https://www.crisistextline.org/texting-in

Substance Abuse and Mental Health Services Administration
- SAMHSA's National Helpline – **1-800-662-HELP (4357)**
- Free, confidential, 24/7, 365-day-a-year treatment referral and information service (in English and Spanish) for individuals and families facing mental and/or substance use disorders.
- https://www.samhsa.gov/find-help/national-helpline

Post-Traumatic Stress Disorder
- NAMI HelpLine at 1-800-950-NAMI (6264)
- info@nami.org
- National Alliance on Mental Illness can answer questions about PTSD or help find support and resources.

Tobacco/Vaping
- 1-800-QUIT-NOW (800-784-8669)
- https://smokefree.gov/

—⟫⟫⟪⟪—

Reflection

- How do you view the issues of tobacco, alcohol, and promiscuity? Does your family background or friend group impact your perception?
- Are you curious about any of these issues? How have you acted on your curiosity?
- What are your core values and beliefs concerning these issues?

- What advice would you give friends or classmates who thought they were addicted to tobacco or alcohol?
- How would you decide if you or someone your love is facing an addiction?

———∾∾∾———

Your Space

If (When) You Mess Up

Dear Auspicious You,

It's not a matter of if you will fall to the bad decisions on campus; it's a matter of when because all of us do. Being human means, just like everyone else, you will mess up even your best laid plans. At some point you will have to deal with shame, embarrassment, and consequences.

You might allow your temper and mouthy attitude to take over and put on a good old-fashioned tantrum in front of the people you are trying to impress. You could also make a huge mistake on a group project and cause grade-turmoil for everyone on your team. On one Thursday night, you might end up drunk, also giving in to promiscuous activities. From seemingly harmless (but still embarrassing) moments to the serious decisions full of destructive consequences, your moments of mishaps are going to happen. Are you prepared to handle and overcome those moments?

If you are feeling overwhelmingly guilty because of past actions, now is the time to assess the situation. Take an objective look at yourself and what happened to you. Did you choose a certain path, or were you forced? Again, look objectively, not making excuses. An open-eyed look at yourself is the first step in overcoming the problems you face.

Maturity occurs when you admit to your own choices and you do not blame others for what happens to you. If you choose to throw a tantrum instead of working through difficult communication problems, choose to watch hours of videos instead of working on your part of a group project, or choose to drink too much and then pair up with someone, then you cannot blame the poor communication, the video, or the alcohol.

First, you must take responsibility for your own actions. Live up to what you selected, as an adult. Running away from actions and blaming others will never free you from the fault and guilt on your shoulders. Once you see yourself as you truly are and accept the responsibility of your own decisions and actions, you will come to understand yourself at a new level. Moving through the uncomfortable assessment of your inner thoughts will offer you time and space to grow away from the unfavorable decisions that landed you into this mess in the first place. You'll be able to walk away from what makes you feel bad much more easily when you do this difficult, inner work and then adjust your actions to match your core values. Basically, learn from your mistakes.

Hear me clearly now. If you're distressed over a situation where you were a victim, you still have plenty of difficult soul-searching to complete, but I encourage you to not do it alone. Go to a trusted adult, such as a campus therapist, and explain how you were a victim and create a plan to work through whatever happened to you. This will take time and assistance from others. You do not have to carry the burden alone. Whether you brought the trouble on yourself or you fell victim to something else, you will be able to emerge on the other side of the troubles with a new perspective, one without doubt, pain, or guilt.

After you measure your progress and move into a more adult version of yourself, you might think your troubles are behind you. Not so. I don't want to add negative thoughts, but after a public moment of messing up, you will have people around you reminding you of the situation.

Some friends will be supportive and help you manage your reactions as you grow up. Other people will wait to see what you do next (at best) or spend their energy gossiping and enjoying your troubles (at worst). The way you respond to the public can take you even farther on the path to arriving as a strong and independent adult.

Most people say they hate drama, but more often than not, the enticing tidbit of news or the scandalous rumor about someone garners much attention. I have witnessed many students claim to hate the drama involved with life, but these same people can't seem to see when they are in the middle of it, which happens to be quite often.

After a rough patch in your life, you will need to remind yourself to be cautious of responding to any negative comments that come your way. I completely understand the desire to defend or explain yourself, but you need to ponder a few main questions. Why are you responding to someone who calls you out for your mistakes? Will your return comments help someone else who is also struggling? Will comments stir up more drama? What are the intentions of the people who are making the comments and asking questions? Do they truly want to know what you learned to join a conversation with you and support you? Do they want inside information to spread all over campus? Will your conversation hurt someone else? Are you telling a story that isn't yours to tell?

I'm not saying to hide away any imperfections and act like nothing happened. I am, however, cautioning you about how and with whom you share your story.

Share in the spirit of honesty and vulnerability in order to communicate how much you learned from your weakness.

Every person on this planet makes poor decisions and ends up hurt and hurting others because of rash behavior. The human condition dictates that we all will fall short of our own expectations as well as the hopes of others.

Don't allow yourself to fall to a back-and-forth quarrel about your situation. An argument won't help anyone, and the ones who want to stir up details again are not truly supportive of you. Make peace with yourself and move on from the situation and any people trying to provoke you. Learn how to close your eyes and breathe deeply to clear your mind, and visualize a place where you feel safe, secure, and happy so that your mind can relax and unwind enough to handle the stress of a situation.

Once you realize how to handle the public perception of your mistakes, you are ready to put the past behind you and figure out how to deal with temptation in the future. Throw away your cigarettes and pour the rest of the alcohol down the drain if those items cause you trouble. Find trusted friends to be your accountability partners and be honest with them.

Forgive yourself.

Even if you make more mistakes and seem to fail with the same issues, keep moving forward and using your coping skills because your life is made of all these beads of experiences. When you thread the beads together, you will see a beautiful string of many-colored events that make you who you are. Embrace each one, but also look to add another bead and then another. After a while, you will see that your string of beads will be filled with more affirming colors with the smooth and shiny surfaces than the dark and sharp ones. Humbly wear your string of beads to remind you of all you have learned and become.

Reflection

- What embarrassing event are you still trying to escape?
- How can you be more honest with yourself concerning this event?
- What is your experience with other people after you make a public mistake?
- What are your coping strategies to restore calm to your mind?
- When you evaluate your decisions, where do you need to improve to not create an error again?

Your Space

PART THREE

Encouragement

Be nice, do good things, make new friends!

Of all the messages that I share with you, these letters full of hope and dreams for your life reflect my belief in you and your future. Every day, I am amazed by the sincerity and courage you show. You are stepping into your adult self as the world is absolutely exploding with new technology, new opportunities, and new connections. You can leave a positive impact more globally than any generation before, and some of you will become an inspiration across lands and oceans. Others will leave your mark on a smaller scale of people, but your ability to be helpful and to serve will mean the whole world to the ones in your circle of influence. I want to help you define your passions and your intended impact as well as to understand that before achieving the highest level of influence on others, you must develop your ethos, your credibility or character. Before you can truly help and influence others, they must believe in your ability. How do you want to use your hands and feet and ethos? I want you to recognize fulfillment in your own lives as you create meaning and purpose for yourselves and others.

—◦∿∿◦—

Identity

Dear Auspicious You,

Who are you? This is such a hard question to answer because most of the time, our perception of identity relies on outside activities, and young adults usually answer by saying common phrases like an athlete, a musician, a nursing major, a BMX racer, or some other noun that defines one part of their lives. The problem with this type of identity association happens because all those answers are dependent upon your abilities to keep doing an external activity. To truly find and verbalize identity, you need to have a bit more inner-vision.

In some of the previous letters, I have encouraged you to ponder and write about your core beliefs. If you haven't done that yet, now is the time. I don't think anyone can truly accept a personal identity until you are able to communicate your value system. Before you think through this task, however, let's specifically define what I mean by a core belief. Most people see these beliefs and values as fundamentally true statements, what you know to be true about the world, other people, and yourself.

Many times, core beliefs develop from childhood because of major events that happened then. This reality also means that core values can be solidified when you are not yet mature and before you think for yourself. To feel completely at ease with yourself, you must ensure that your core beliefs actually do belong to you, not your parents, older family members, or group of friends.

A smart young woman named Lucy was feeling disconcerted, not able to relax or enjoy looking forward to her future. Her anxiety seemed to stem from her move to college, but she couldn't figure out why she was so worried. She enjoyed the difficult high school classes and felt prepared for the challenge, and she was excited about living on her own. Even as she hauled her tubs and boxes into her dorm room, she couldn't shake this weird feeling. What was wrong?

Lucy's year started much more smoothly than my freshman year of college, and she enjoyed her interpersonal relationship class very much. Her experience in class challenged her to reflect on life, her decisions, and her beliefs in ways that she hadn't allowed herself to think before. She and I shared a long conversation covering topics from the importance of education and servanthood to spirituality, body modifications, and parenting styles. Lucy shared with me that through these new views from her class, she was able to recognize where she simply accepted her family's belief systems without assessing her own. Eventually, she attributed her unsettled feelings to never personally doing the internal work of grasping how she, as an adult, viewed different core beliefs.

She learned that she did share many core beliefs with her parents and siblings, but other ideas were emerging as she matured. For example, Lucy had several first-hand spiritual experiences, so her belief in God was strong and vital to her. However, some of her beliefs about conflict management were not as steadfast.

Her father tended to discipline with passive-aggressive comments and actions, which hurt Lucy's feelings many times when she was younger. She didn't know how to make him happy, or even why he was upset, but Lucy picked up on his angry tone of voice. For a long while, Lucy accepted and believed that being antagonistic and making snide comments to show displeasure was the best way to deal with conflict.

After her roommate, boyfriend, and a group of girlfriends continually struggled with Lucy's passive aggressive manners, her roommate finally sat down with her and asked how they could better communicate. This precious conversation along with the new information from her college course opened Lucy's eyes to the behavior. She was taken aback by her roommate's straightforward approach to solving the problem. After the conversation, Lucy worked to be concise about her feelings. When her roommate asked if Lucy could help keep their apartment clean by taking out the trash when the sack was full, Lucy tried to no longer get angry and pile the trash higher. Lucy's core belief from her young adult self didn't match her dad's core belief about solving conflicts. Once she recognized this disconnect, she was able to feel more settled and less anxious about her own identity. This type of self-awareness will help you recognize your own core beliefs, which will make your search for adult identity more fruitful.

From this solid footing of understanding your set of beliefs, you can then look at the rules you set for your life. Are you living like a fifth grader at home alone for the first time who just found a gallon of ice cream and a spoon? While the house rules that applied to you when you were a young high school freshman have changed, do you still have rules to follow? Have you found new freedom that you can't handle? How do you monitor yourself to live by your core values?

Proof that you have a solid understanding of who you are comes from your ability to monitor and motivate yourself. Young adults like you find a move from high school to college allows you to develop your own thoughts of what's important instead of depending on someone older to tell you how to think and behave. Developing your identity as an adult, you can create the new version of yourself instead of playing the role of the high school version of you.

Solving your own problems is another key for solidifying your identity. You can improve your understanding of who you are by being more self-sufficient, without letting parents solve problems for you. Yes, talk to parents and get advice, but do not depend on your parents to solve problems *for* you. Make your own decisions. Solve your own problems. Work out your conflicts with the people involved. Developing a strong sense of identity can't happen if you complain and tattle to your parents and expect them to negotiate solutions between you and your friends, teachers, coaches, or employers. One of the best feelings is relying on your own courage and resiliency to stand up to and solve conflicts.

If I return to the beginning question, do you now have a better idea of how to answer it? At least have a stronger sense of how to determine your answer? Let's find out.

Who are you?

I hope you can now answer in a more complex and layered response instead of just saying a student, a ballerina, or a rugby player. Your ability to be self-aware will help you gain a solid sense of who you are and who you want to become. As you move through more adult situations, you will see how to juggle the different hats you must wear without feeling torn between who you are with your friends or in a classroom.

You already know that as an adult, you will present yourself in various situations, which each call for you to almost be a different persona. If you are babysitting, you must be mindful of safety and presenting yourself as loving, caring, firm, and fun. After you are finished with the job, you might meet friends for a study session where you will need to know high-level math or science concepts as well as how to stay on topic to study well. Later that evening, you might grab a quick bite to eat with roommates where you can laugh and be silly. Before going to sleep, you might answer a phone call from a grandparent where you transform back into the kid who loves to chatter on while Grandma dotes on you and hangs on your every word. How can all these roles fit into one person in one day?

Think about it. You do it all the time. Successful communicators assess situations and can apply their manners to fit the expectations of cultural norms. You might notice trouble with establishing your identity if you are unable to move seamlessly from one role into another. The core of who you are cannot change. Whether you are attending a party or chatting with your grandma, you should be the same core person.

If you are pretending to be someone you are not in one of the scenarios, putting on a false front, your anxiety will grow. When you figure out who you are, you will be confident to hold those beliefs and not waver even when you are presenting yourself in different circumstances. You also need to understand that when you have many roles and jobs to perform, these various parts of you must rely on your core beliefs when tragedy or hardship happens. When you are a young adult student juggling many responsibilities, you might feel pressed to the limit. Then, a hardship such as a job loss or a car wreck might make you feel like you simply cannot take one more hit.

If you don't have a core belief system and a true sense of who you are, these tragic moments will affect you even more. Instead of becoming tangled in the problems of not being able to handle the tough moments, you can rely on your value system to guide your actions and methods to solve problems.

Furthermore, understanding your identity will help you find a new level of success that might be eluding you right now. With so many young adults, comfortable situations are easy to handle, but any stressors throw them into a quandary. I know you want to be successful and make a positive impact on the people around you, and I also know how you feel the stomach flips and sweaty palms associated with facing difficulty standing in the way of your influence.

Knowing yourself and your core identity will allow you to be effective with book smarts and life smarts. You can develop great relationships with family, friends, teachers, and employers when you work on the soft skills of life such as effectively communicating, looking for multiple ways to solve problems, working in a group, being self-motivated, working through the end of a project, finishing strong, not leaving work with loose ends, cleaning up after yourself, never saying a task is too hard, never giving up. Your assuredness about your identity allows you to be less emotional when you need to be strong and find internal fortitude when problems arise. You will be able to grit your teeth and make it to the end of a situation.

Is this who you are?

As you answer this question please remember that I am proud of you for completing this tough, internal work. Developing a core identity takes much effort and revision. You have the ability to hone your identity and advance as a young adult who's able to balance your family legacy and your emerging adult beliefs as you remain steadfast in the face of many situations. You will also be proud of the labor as you complete this important search for yourself.

—⚬⚬⚬—

Reflection

- How do you define a core belief?
- What values do you share with your family and friends?
- With which beliefs do you deviate from your family and friends?

- How do you want to expand your previous high school identity as you grow?
- How do you juggle the different hats that you wear each day?
- Do you have the grit needed to finish tasks strongly? How can you improve?

———∿∿∿———

Your Space

Uncertainty

Dear Auspicious You,

Even the best, brightest, and most talented students second guess themselves and revert to talking about how stressed they are or how they don't know what to do when a situation gets difficult. Is there any way I can coax you into accepting uneasiness more easily? Most likely, your first instinct concerning a walk outside of your comfort zone is rejecting the new situation. When you don't know what to do or say, you probably want to hide.

If you have responsibilities coming at you from all directions, you might end up holding your head in your hands and spouting off trite phrases: "I don't have time!" "My professor didn't explain how to do it, so I got a poor grade." "No one understands." "My group members are not taking the project seriously, and I have to do everything all by myself!" "I'm too tired." "I have to work, so I can't volunteer."

Sometimes these statements are true. Most of the time, these statements feel true, but are just excuses for not preparing properly or for being selfish or for not wanting to face ambiguous situations. I know you like specific guidelines and knowing the answer. You want to be sure that 2+2=4. But, sometimes, challenges are bigger than one correct answer. Sometimes, you must be willing to enjoy the space outside of your comfort zone. I encourage you to embrace and seek out uncertainty because in the state of being unsure, you will grow the most. Be ok with not knowing how and not knowing the answer.

If I could give my younger self any piece of advice, I think I'd choose this one. I loved security. I mean, *loved* it. I needed to know that my actions and words and school work and beliefs were acceptable and within the limits set by my family and friends. If I felt uncertain, I readjusted my course to move back into the safety of knowing the answers. I'm not sure how this flaw in my personality started, but it might have been on my first birthday.

One of my family's traditions includes providing a small cake for a child's first birthday. We strip the kid down to the diaper, put the cake in front of him, and get the cameras ready. Some of our favorite memories and pictures happen in these moments, and even though no one remembers our own specific event, the pictures that remain and the family stories we tell about the cakes draw us together.

My first birthday cake was a tiny circle cake with one lit candle in the middle. As my dad ran the 35-millimeter camera recording my every move, I became obsessed with the flame. I tried to grab the flame with my chubby little hand. When you watch this silent movie, you see my hand going for the flame and my mom's graceful hand intervening, pushing mine safely away from the heat. She pushes me away once and then twice. My stubborn streak was obviously going strong even as a one-year-old because you can see me reaching to grab the flame a third time.

Now, at this point, some parents might go ahead and blow out the candle, removing the danger and possible pain-producing heat. Not in my house. You know how much I love my parents and how much I realize their absolute wisdom as I age. They wanted to protect me, but they also wanted me to learn about the world and to be independent. Back then, my parents didn't remove obstacles. On the third time when I reached for the flame, my mom just sat there. Of course, Dad kept filming. My fingers wiggled toward the flame and closed around it. Instantly, my face crumpled into frowning wrinkles, and I let loose a wail. Tears flowed. Mom came quickly to the rescue, and in no time, I was soothed back into calmness. Then, I earnestly started digging into the cake.

My candle lesson might be the time where I learned to be uncertain and learned to only grab for something safe. This isn't the lesson my parents intended, but I lived with hesitation for as far back as I can remember. I wanted approval, and I aimed to please as many people as I could. Compliments and encouragement were like oxygen! I did all kinds of activities when I knew my family would be there to help me succeed. I was independent and confident when I knew I couldn't mess up too badly.

However, if I wasn't sure I could succeed with a task, I wouldn't do it. I didn't try out for 5th grade cheerleading because I was scared to be in front of the student body. (Back then, all the way up through high school, our tryout happened in front of everyone at school, and the students voted for the girls they wanted. It was terrifying for me.) As I grew and as my parents continued teaching me about determination and taking risks when I had to depend on myself, I became more comfortable. I did try out and ended up on the cheer team for grades six through twelve. I got a job as a waitress, a babysitter, and a sales clerk. I learned to push past the uncertainty and reach for the goals that I wanted. This is the lesson from my parents. After pushing through a painful experience, I was able to enjoy something sweet.

Still, I could have reached even farther out of my comfort zone. My college roommate, Maria, accepted an internship at Disney World in Florida, and she experienced many amazing moments. Why didn't I travel somewhere to do my student teaching? Fear of the unknown. Other friends traveled to different countries for work and pleasure, and some went on mission trips or served in the military. I planted myself in southern Indiana and stayed here. Even though I'm no longer the baby reaching for the candle, sometimes I still feel tied to expectations and making people happy. You know, writing these letters to you is a giant leap out of my comfort zone. However, my time writing to you invigorates me more than I can explain. I want to share how much I treasure you and how much I want to encourage you to take the leaps and risks so you can feel the excitement of a life lived fully. I wish I hadn't waited so long, and I want you to stop being uncertain now.

You are facing a time of your life with more uncertainty than ever before. As a young adult, you will live away from your parents while being responsible for your own grades and study habits. Living in a new place, learning how to drive in a new city, and deciding where to buy groceries are big changes. Then you will be adding on the stress of making decisions about your future and trying to find the perfect fit for you in a career and a like-minded group of people. All these tasks are risky and frightening, but you can be successful.

Examine yourself to see if the statements you tend to say quite often truly reflect actual events or if you are making excuses for not facing new experiences. Pinpoint exactly why you hesitate to act or become involved with opportunities. Are you allowing your family or significant other to make choices for you? Have you lost the courage to explore? Are you just going through the daily motions because you don't want to fail or upset anyone?

Your hesitation must stop. It's time for you to reach beyond your fears and worries to see how far your potential can take you. Dig into your cake!

—◦◦◦—

Reflection

- What are your usual statements when facing uncertainty and uneasiness?
- Are these true or excuses?
- When have you held back from an adventure because you felt uncertain or scared?
- When did you bravely face uncertainty and achieve your goal?
- How can you remember this courage for the next task that challenges you?

———∞∞———

Your Space

Trust Your Authentic Gut

Dear Auspicious You,

Almost every one of my letters to you emphasizes the theme of knowing yourself and learning who you are and what you believe. In relationships and in times of stress, understanding yourself, your motives, and your needs becomes the difference between successfully developing or floundering around trying to make decisions. Knowing yourself is important, for sure, but the knowledge alone is not enough for you to create a healthy and fulfilled life. Let me explain.

By this point in your educational journey, you have listened to many teachers describe persuasion and persuasive writing. Every high school sophomore writing curriculum I've ever seen includes a section discussing how to convince an audience using various stylistic elements and rhetorical devises with the goal of persuading them to accept your viewpoint.

When I teach this unit, like many educators, I add concepts that push beyond merely accepting a belief using a very specific example. High school students are ready for a reliable car. They want the license, the wheels, and the freedom, so I use the subject to my advantage when I teach persuasion.

In my lesson I have the class brainstorm many reasons their parents should provide them with a newer, more reliable car.

We talk about logical fallacies and work to eliminate them from their arguments. The students usually present valid evidence, complete with statistical research, why reliable vehicles would make not only their own lives, but also their parents' lives better. By the time the students are writing their logical and emotional appeals, there isn't a parent in a hundred-mile radius who would disagree with them.

If the students have the goal of persuading the parents to simply agree with their belief, they succeed every time. The problem, however, arises because even though the parents agree, they don't place a new set of car keys in the hands of the students. Actually, in all the years I have taught this lesson, not one parent has ever coughed up the keys to a new car. Making someone agree with your belief is progress, but a belief is not enough. To truly witness success when you persuade someone, you need to see actions. The same concept applies to your knowing and understanding yourself.

I will be so pleased if my letters to you are helpful and lead you to complete the tough inner work of discovering who you are, how you deal with relationships, what kinds of activities make you look forward to the future, or when you need to set new goals. Still, just *knowing* new information about yourself will leave you empty and conflicted unless you *act* on what you know. You will have to be brave enough to stand up for yourself when you are making your life's decisions.

When you recognize your core beliefs and goals, you do not need anyone to make choices or decisions for you. Parents, roommates, friends, family, and teachers all have advice, but you can't pretend to be someone you are not or to enjoy some activity that you do not just to please someone else. You must gain confidence in your authentic voice.

Time and time again, young adults get right to the edge of a new venture and then hit the brakes. A talented young man named Todd enjoyed science classes all through high school. He took every chemistry, biology, and physics class he could, and he did very well. The subject came easy to him. He also found interests in working with local non-profit organizations and felt satisfied when his work in this capacity helped other people.

When it was time to declare his major at college, he picked a science field and even won a prestigious scholarship from the science department of his university. About two months before he graduated from high school, however, he started second-guessing his decision. He didn't think he was good enough with scientific research. He wasn't sure if he really loved the subject enough to study it every day of his life for the entire rest of his life. He thought about his humanitarian efforts and remembered how much he loved interacting with people. If he followed the call of chemistry or biology on his life, he would make good money, but he was afraid after all the schooling, he would lose his passion for the disadvantaged because he would be caught up in the rat race of jumping through the next hoop and feeling exhausted.

Todd worried so much he had trouble sleeping and announced to his family that he was changing his major. His parents were stunned. He blindsided them by even thinking about ditching the dream of a profession in the science field as well as the scholarship from the science department before he attended one college class. He didn't share any of his concerns with them before this announcement, so he had no one with whom he could explore these thoughts. Luckily, Todd's parents helped him work through these concerns, and he felt comfortable accepting the major and the scholarship as he began his college career.

Other students have experienced the same phenomenon. A talented musician hesitated to pursue a career in the music industry because she was afraid to lose her passion if she had to work in the field as a job. One student who showed promise as a computer technician changed his life plan because the scholarship he needed to pay for schooling wasn't awarded to him. Another young man who had a 3.8 GPA and only one semester left of college wanted to change his plan because, ultimately, he was frustrated. He didn't see the purpose in a few of his major classes, so he was prepared to change it altogether and start over so he wouldn't feel trapped in his current major.

These are all true stories. If you are questioning your future, you are not alone. How can you be sure you are following the appropriate career plan?

Most people ask what you want to be or what area you want to study. They ask about your likes and dislikes and want to dig into results from interest inventories you've taken. Some of these career planning tools do not cost any money and can offer valuable information at times. They can help you decide if you have the same interests and preferences as other people who are in certain fields.

Still, my biggest problem with these assessments comes from the blanket-effect they seem to create. I Googled "free interest inventory" and ended up with over 200,000,000 hits. You can find a different survey on every virtual corner offering a way for you to answer questions to figure out your life's purpose. The tests ask questions with no right or wrong answer, and the ones I have taken seem to ask the same question phrased differently many times over. By the time I am just a few pages into the assessment, I can tell if the question pertains to construction, science, math, healthcare, or education.

I am not a psychologist or counselor, so I do not know the finer points about these inventories, but I do see some flaws that come along with the career information. For example, what if it asks you how much you like to take apart a robot to see how the pieces work? If you've never done that before, how do you know if you like it? You have a presupposed idea about the mechanics of disassembling a robot, but you have no real background to base your answer on experience. How is that valid?

Also, the categories seem very broad. I know myself very well by now. I am a caregiver, a teacher, a writer, a listener, a question-asker, a speaker, a leader. All these skills perfectly fit with being a mom, librarian, teacher, and author. However, according to an interest inventory I recently completed, these skills also could lead me toward life as a human resources manager (Maybe, but don't they deal with insurance and payroll?), advertising and marketing (Ick! I bet they have to do math.), or a top executive (Be the boss? No thanks.) If students use the results as a guide, fine, but the interest inventories make me a bit nervous when students base decisions from their results alone. That's why I don't ask the questions about what you like or what you want to be.

The best question I can ask when a student bemoans not knowing exactly which direction to take is this one: How do you want to serve?

When you get lost in the activity of helping someone else, you will feel fulfilled, positive, and joyful. What activities make you not care what time it is and make you forget to check your phone? When do you feel you are making life better for someone else? What skill do you use that allows you to have complete concentration when you are working? What talents are you developing when your mind focuses on the task and lets the rest of the world and all its trials fall away? Which situations let you feel satisfied and like you are contributing to the greater good?

Your answers to these questions will not depend on an interest inventory or career planning questionnaire. Instead, these answers depend on life experiences. To know yourself enough to answer these, you must place yourself in various situations.

I'm sure you've heard the well-known phrase that rings of truth: experience is the best teacher. When you complete many different types of tasks, you will learn so much about yourself. Personally, I have a vertical imbalance in my vision, so I cannot follow a spreadsheet line across a page without a guide and a whole lot of squinting. Plus, I am not good at math beyond the basics. It's just not my cup of tea. When I work on budgets for the libraries, time slows to a crawl, and I look over every entry multiple times to make sure that I'm not making a monetary mistake that will affect my school. It's almost misery for me. I feel differently about budgets and math than I do about a fun event like research instruction because I have experienced the tasks and my responses to them.

Here's a little insight as well. Just because I don't like doing purchasing and budget work doesn't mean I can skip that part of my job. I continue to keep records updated and work with our treasurers. Also, I am not about to give up my librarianship or teaching because some of my stressful responsibilities are ones I do not enjoy. You will never find a career, profession, or job that offers you only tasks you love. All work has duties to cause you the almost-misery moments, so you can't quit serving based on one small portion you don't like. Look at the bigger picture.

The hardest part of being a wonderful, bright, and talented young adult like you is that you are skilled in many areas. You have multiple interests, and you are not sure which one will end up being the best fit for a life-time career. Being smart and effective is biting you in the hind end, right? Well, not really.

Explore the question about service. If you are truly uncertain about a major, do not declare one hastily. Go into your college experience with an exploratory major and check into various options. You will most likely have an idea of an area of interest such as healthcare or business. The counselors in the undecided major are experts with helping you have different experiences and explore many options of service to find the area where you lose track of time and feel part of a movement bigger than yourself. If you are in a major where you feel unsure, you need to assess whether you aren't comfortable with all the responsibilities or with only a few that stretch you beyond the comfort zone you enjoy.

One of my wise students wrote a poem to his future self. The assignment called for an elegy, and he wrote a reminder to himself about what he didn't want to lose in the future. He wants his future self to still enjoy nature and the excitement of discovering new truths about our world. He wants to rein himself back if he gets too caught up in the circle of work, money, prestige, promotions, and the like. He never wants to lose the importance of family and close friends. He still wants to sing for joy and allow himself to feel sorrow. He doesn't want a career to make him so serious that he loses the ability to see the beauty of the world through clear eyes. Isn't that awesome? If you are struggling with what you want to be and do in your future, find your authentic voice and follow your gut instinct. To be sure about your authentic gut, I encourage you to do the following: answer how you want to serve and write a letter to your future self about what you do not ever want to lose. These two activities will allow you to see what is truly important to you, and your decision will feel more settled in your heart.

—◦◦◦◦—

Reflection

- How do your actions prove that you know your authentic self?
- Why do you question the plan that you've currently set for yourself?

- What's your experience with an interest inventory?
- When do you lose track of time?
- How do you want to serve?

———∿∿∿———

Your Space

Look Out Your Window

Dear Auspicious You,

A human develops along a specific progression of stages and timelines. Freud, Piaget, Erikson, and many other scientists provide theories detailing this process of human cognitive development. The theories, and the people behind them, are fascinating to study because you can place yourself in their models and analyze the plausibility of each. Classes that delve into this subject matter have always been entertaining and challenging as they allow us to see how scientists prove and discredit the famous theories as well as introduce new ones.

As I have gotten older and have watched my students and my own children go through the stages of development, I can verify some of the scientists' work and question others. I have been a witness over and over to an absolute key to maturity, joy, and fulfillment, and at first, my theory (which isn't new or earth-shaking by any means) seems counter-intuitive.

To truly focus on your self-improvement, your own maturity, and your heart's contentment, after you work through defining your core inner beliefs, you will have to look outside of yourself to turn those beliefs into action. You need to give your energy and talents to an effort that helps someone else if you want to advance yourself.

Many of my letters to you share this same idea because taking your focus off yourself and looking outside of your personal window offers you a new perspective. You will see others who need you, find a place to use your skills for good, feel valuable and competent, and create plans for making a bigger difference in your world. All your best work will happen when you are not concerned about you.

Think of a flashlight. When you hold the light close to the floor, the beam of light is narrow and short, and it doesn't give off much of a helpful glow at all. However, when you continually move the light away from the floor, the brightness expands. To see the biggest impact of a flashlight, you can point it out in front of you, illuminating lots of space for the benefit of many. Your attention to others uses the same concepts. Being selfish and holding down your influence does not create light or helpful situations for others.

However, like a flashlight being drawn away from the floor, when you expand your awareness of others and start to look beyond your own activities, problems, and desires, you will feel like you are a part of something bigger than yourself. You will realize your development as a human is progressing. Even when you start to notice other people and how you can help them, you will have moments of selfishness that will zoom your light right back to a pinpoint on the floor. As you grow, the goal is for those moments to be fewer and farther away from each other.

Finally, when you can shine your flashlight beam ahead of you, scanning for how to assist and fulfill your goals in making a difference for someone else, your circle of light will be at its peak. In those times you will find more meaning in life, and you will be excited to proceed. Studying and working on a project will not be tedious when you are creating a device to help a child with a disability experience life more easily and fully. If you are organizing an event to benefit a campus need, such as availability of service animals, you will have more compelling thoughts which will lead to better conversations with others. When someone asks how you are doing, you won't answer with the standard young adult quip of "I'm tired." Instead, you will have details to share and brainstorming ideas to discuss.

Do you see how by looking beyond yourself, you open life up to new people, places, and conversations? You won't be a boring date when you have interests to discuss. In job interviews or in fitness class, others will notice your zest for life and will want to interact with you.

If my explanation of a helping theory makes sense to you, then why aren't more young adults like you happy and fulfilled as they work to benefit a greater good? Honestly? Getting out of your own head is not easy. The best intentions can go sour and not happen when your emotions hold your flashlight beam to the floor. Sometimes life gets too big with problems, and it's hard to see beyond them. Internal issues cause trouble with organization, procrastinating, and being able to let go of a situation that makes you sad or angry.

In the past years, I have taught two very bright students who had trouble getting out of their own heads. One student, Samuel, owned the most stuffed backpack I have ever seen. I think the guy lived out of that thing. He carried books and papers from every class in the bag, but all the pieces were crammed inside with no organization. Pages from science classes were folded up with English assignments, and project notes from government spilled out of his math book. Samuel was always respectful and worked very hard in class. Still, I sensed something else was going on inside of his mind. He had a reserved personality at school, and I wondered if he stuffed emotions into his heart just like the items in his backpack. He had so much to offer the world, but I'm not certain he allowed himself to look out the window to see the possibilities. Much of what happens to us is out of our control, and when problems are running rampant at home or work, I know even keeping a backpack organized is a trial, so my asking you to look for someone else's problems to take on as your own might seem like too much.

Being unable to brush off conflict is another issue facing many young adults. Paula, one of my previous students, faced a situation I've seen in dozens of people. She simply couldn't let go of being angry. One of her previous friends triggered the reaction, and if they had a conflict, the floodgates opened, and she was white-hot mad in an instant. She turned over power to the other person so many times by getting emotional, and I wanted to help her see past the hurt feelings of the moment. But when Paula felt hurt, she couldn't look past herself even though she was a natural leader and able to be an effective project manager as well as a worker.

Going from a high school adolescent to a mature adult isn't easy, and you might be thinking you simply can't assist another person when you are feeling overwhelmed or angry all the time. Still, I promise an effective way to get from point A to point B is by looking to help someone else. You need to see how your core beliefs boost your potential to help others and be truly happy and fulfilled in your life at this moment without having to wait for a diploma to get life started. You can start with small tasks. Look around and notice other people. Give smiles and sincere compliments.

From this beginning, you can look for other ways to help people or animals. Do you notice an elderly person struggling with opening a heavy door? Go help. Does a crying baby in the line at the grocery store cause the mom to seem overwhelmed? Give her some encouragement by helping her load the groceries in her car. Did another student give a particularly good presentation in class? Tell him why you enjoyed the talk and ask some questions.

When you feel comfortable with these types of low-commitment steps, you can find more tasks to assist people. Your intrinsic motivation will increase each time you step outside of yourself because you will feel more connected to others. You will get a dose of feel-good hormones and want to do more.[15] Participating in social behavior that comes from volunteering or working with a team to solve a real problem will also improve your personal situation. Excitement for a task breeds excitement for the whole project as well as the people who are impacted. You can't go wrong when you look out your window to find a need and meet it.

—◦◦◦—

Reflection

- When do you tend to place all your focus on yourself?
- How does this tendency cause conflict for you?
- In what ways could you see the helping behaviors improving your life?
- Where should you begin your own version of helping behaviors? Why?

—◦◦◦—

Your Space

Explore

Dear Auspicious You,

You have peeked out your window and now see a big, exciting world out there. Now is the time to explore! As an adult, you will be spending more time alone than ever before, but you still can find so much to see and do. Some of the best adventures can happen when you get brave enough to not only notice the world beyond yourself, but also to take some action. I learned this lesson as a kindergartener.

I was given a pony named Trouble when I was in preschool, and throughout the year, we grew comfortable with one another. In the beginning I was too little to lift the saddle, so a family member would saddle him while I put on the bridle. Then Trouble and I usually took off to ride around the barn lot, the arena, or in the meadow close to the barn. I became more confident of my riding ability. However, I ended up in a particularly awful predicament on a beautiful fall afternoon.

When I had been riding for a few months, I decided to saddle Trouble by myself and ride to the big pear tree in the middle of the hay field. The tree was a favorite spot of mine, especially in the fall when the pears were ripe and the colors were beautiful. Riding Trouble out there would be so much faster than walking, so (without telling anyone where I was going), I turned Trouble toward the field. With the nervous energy coursing through me because of riding where I hadn't before, I didn't notice my new beagle puppy following us.

When we neared the pear tree, I was feeling great! My plan was to find a few pears to take back and share with my family. However, as we got closer and closer, I could hear the buzz that scared me more than any other—bees. I instantly tightened up every muscle in my kindergarten body. All pony riders know the human dictates the mood of the animal, so my signals were instantly sending off messages to Trouble that I sensed danger. He started to whinny, stomp, and buck. I was hanging on for dear life when I noticed our next problem. The puppy thought we were playing, and she started to prance around, nipping at Trouble's hooves.

This new commotion was more than Trouble could handle, and he bolted—not in a nice canter that entertained me. He was scared, angry, and on his way out of that hay field at a dead run! I could not do anything to stop him, so I just clung to the saddle, which was a good plan until it started to slip. Slowly at first and then in one big twist, I ended up moving down the right side of my pony.

Before I knew what had happened, I was literally under Trouble. As such a young kid, I could not think fast enough to plan an escape from this frantic ride. My feet were still in the stirrups somehow, and through leg grips and hands on the saddle horn, I hung precariously from his belly, bouncing like a loose tail light wire on the flatbed trailer.

The beagle continued chasing us, as her hunting instincts kicked into gear. Her "encouragement" made Trouble run all the faster and made me lose my grip on the saddle. As I slipped closer to the ground, I noticed hard sticks hitting me in the face. The leftovers from the hay harvest had turned brown and inflexible in the autumn sun, and those stray pieces of hay slashed me in the face and neck like whips. I could no longer hold on and take such a beating to my face, so I simply let go. I did not realize the danger of getting trampled by hooves, but luckily, I did not have to deal with that because I bounced and rolled off to the side. When I finally stopped, my dad was somehow standing over me.

Apparently, Dad watched as I tumbled from Trouble and sprinted as fast as he could to my rescue. Luckily, I was able to hug Trouble's belly long enough to have him slow down a bit before I let go. I suffered no broken bones—just bruises and scratches. When Dad carried me back to the barn lot, Trouble and the pup were there, waiting and staring at me almost as if they were asking where I'd been. Needless to say, Dad made me get back on and ride around the arena. And, to this day, I am still not sure if my mom knew the whole story. Poor Trouble might have been a goner if she had known.

Our trip to the pear tree allowed Trouble and me to know each other even more, and we continued to get along well. I am so thankful I was not hurt and Dad did not sell Trouble to the glue factory. From this early adventure, I learned the value of exploring. Even with the physical bruises, a spark ignited inside of me.

I bravely started walking every trail I could find and spent hours by myself in the woods. My exploration led me to the river, the pasture full of cows, fun grapevine swings, and a sandy beach by the creek. I could not get enough of the solitude and the benefits of nature, and my love for the outdoors continues to this day. I also found the confidence to face the unknown and the thinking skills to figure out the world around me. In fact, my time in nature when I was so young stayed with me, and I am certain that it subconsciously led me to the healing time I spent in the camper a few years later. You remember how important that time was in my maturing.

What was your first adventure? Was it a life-changing experience like mine? Do your adventures let you see a bigger world you still need to explore? After you realize you have potential to be an active participant in the world, an excitement will rise in you, and you should capitalize on the excitement and momentum. As a modern student, you have opportunities to travel as sports ambassadors or missionaries, and you have places to volunteer where you can truly relate to others. You do not have to wait to be older to accomplish your desire to see the world outside of your own campus.

You can reclaim the sense of endless possibilities you gained from the solo adventures of your youth. Don't wait until you graduate or until you are in your own apartment or until you get your first "real" job. Do it now!

Remember you are good company and remember the fun you can have when you get out and *do* something. Put the phone down. Quit looking at posts and videos. You can find an activity and participate to begin the process of rediscovering the kid inside of you.

Speaking of your past self, would he be happy with you? Would she approve of your sliding into a closed-off attitude and self-centered mindset against the rest of the world? I don't think so, either. It's time to start exploring again and insert yourself into the bigger world. Even though your first steps will probably be by yourself, eventually you will find awesome people who will help you, and the excitement will keep you from a life of boring routine. You will cherish your new adventures just as much as the ones you had when you were little, and the opportunities you have as a young adult will offer abundant life to you as you share it with others.

—⚬⚬⚬—

Reflection

- What were the sights, sounds, and smells associated with your first adventure?
- How did that adventure change you?
- Where would you love to explore?
- How can you turn your focus to other people as you take adventures?

———◈———

Your Space

Auspicious You

Dear Auspicious You,

Even though I defined the word in my preface and addressed you as "auspicious" in the salutation of each letter, do you really know what it means yet? Can you define how you are auspicious and know how I see you fitting the description perfectly? Following a good conclusion strategy, let's define this important term again, here at the end of my letters.

Auspicious is an adjective describing you. You are fortunate, bright, hopeful, encouraging, and prosperous. You are also auspicious because you are characterized by success and full of promise. At this very moment, your life as a young adult will lead you into an advantageous future where you will be beneficial to others.

———

I am so proud of you!
I am so excited to hear where your adventures and your desire to serve takes you!

———

Hopefully, my letters have helped you recognize the areas of relationships, stressful situations, and empowering moments where you can now also see yourself as auspicious. Stepping into a new season of life is always a bit scary, and if you were not a little unsure, I would be worried you were not paying attention. On the other hand, you are at a perfect time in your life to make some decisions about yourself. Do you know your own strengths, talents, and ambitions? Do you recognize ways to stay motivated and serve in your group of people and beyond?

A big change from teenage years into young adult years happens with the encouragement you receive. As a teen, you have friends, family, and teachers who stay connected with your life and activities. They know your assignments and your struggles. They see your personal statistics such as your grades and your bank account. When a teenager slips a little and needs a push, usually someone in the group is only a small step away and will jump into a conversation to scold, refocus, or reassure.

As a young adult, you need to monitor your own motivation and choices. An auspicious person like you will not have difficulty seeing the signs and adjusting your own behavior as needed. You will stay focused on the goal ahead of you and connect yourself to the people who will serve with you.

After reading all of my letters, you should be able to answer my last question without anxiety or worry. You can remember the advice I've given you to relax and focus on the actions and decisions which bring you peace. You should know by now that the answer to my final question will be a work in progress, like a working thesis. The answer will change and grow with you. Revisions of your answer should show deeper levels of commitment and wisdom. You should be excited to discuss your answer with loved ones and others who can help you get there. Are you ready?

—⟪∿∿⟫—

What is your mission for the next step of your life,
and how will you ensure your success?

—⟪∿∿⟫—

Your Space

APPENDICES

Information: Blessing Hearts

When You Go There

I don't have to tell you that life can
creep into the plans you've made for the
future. You have known pain and loss
and fear when your blueprint for
what's next fell apart...broken
into lines and numbers.
But look at you now.
In past trials you created mistakes,
but that's how you got here.
Now you're ready to go there.
This next step looms giant-sized on
your horizon and carries such heavy
weights of independence, priorities, decisions,
preparation: creating you all over again.
You are ready to go there.
So much prepares you to take these steps.
You know to acknowledge the past, but
not to live back then.
You have God-given talents. I see them.
When you get there, use your gifts...
let them flow freely, expanding into life.
When you face the darkness again, and

you will, feel my confidence in you.
A few breaths and a bit of chocolate
wouldn't hurt, either. Smile anyway.
You'll be ready to go there, too.
Leaving here. Moving toward your destiny.
Remember you are ready
when you go there.

-----Lori Vandeventer, May 2009

Written for my Seniors of
Eastern Greene High School
Class of 2009

End Notes

[1]   Crowe, Cameron, director. *We Bought a Zoo*, performed by Matt Damon (2011; USA: Twentieth Century Fox, 2012), Film.

~A powerful quote from this film is delivered by Matt Damon as he plays Benjamin Mee: "You know, sometimes all you need is twenty seconds of insane courage. Just literally twenty seconds of just embarrassing bravery. And I promise you, something great will come of it."

[2]   Campanile, Guy and Andrew Bast, producers. "What Is 'Brain Hacking'? Tech Insiders on Why You Should Care." CBS News. April 9, 2017. Accessed June 04, 2019. https://www.cbsnews.com/news/brain-hacking-tech-insiders-60-minutes/. (Video: https://www.youtube.com/watch?v=awAMTQZmvPE)

Deibert, Ronald J. "The Road to Digital Unfreedom: Three Painful Truths About Social Media." *Journal of Democracy* 30, no. 1 (2019): 25-39. https://muse.jhu.edu/ (accessed June 3, 2019).

Price, Catherine, "Trapped – The Secret Ways Social Media Is Built to Be Addictive (And What You Can Do to Fight Back)," October 29, 2018, *Science Focus*, BBC, https://www.sciencefocus.com/future-technology/trapped-the-secret-ways-social-media-is-built-to-be-addictive-and-what-you-can-do-to-fight-back/ (accessed June 3, 2019).

3   De Hoyos, Brandon. "Know Your Rights: Sexting Laws by State in the US." Lifewire. April 15, 2019. Accessed June 04, 2019. https://www.lifewire.com/sexting-laws-in-united-states-1949957.

4   Goodchild van Hilten, Lucy. "Sexting Coercion Is on the Rise – and Can Be as Traumatic as Partner Violence." Elsevier Connect. June 5, 2015. Accessed June 04, 2019. https://www.elsevier.com/connect/sexting-coercion-is-on-the-rise-and-can-be-as-traumatic-as-partner-violence.

5   Wilson, Brett. Senior pastor/teacher at Cross Lane Community Church. Terre Haute, IN. http://clcchurch.com/about-us/staff.

6   Medina, John. *Brain Rules: 32 Principles for Surviving and Thriving at Work, Home and School*. Seattle, WA: Pear Press, 2014.

7   A T-Chart is an analysis tool that allows for a compare and contrast of objects focusing on the features being analyzed. I always use a T-Chart because the evidence is automatically organized.

Smekens, Kristina. "Plan Text-to-Text Comparisons with a T-Chart." Smekens Education

Solutions. March 28, 2012. Accessed June 07, 2019. https://www.smekenseducation.com/ Plan-TexttoText-Comparisons-wit.html.

8   Dillard, Annie. *An American Childhood.* New York: Harper Perennial, 2013.

9   Vibrant Emotional Health. *National Suicide Prevention Lifeline.* Substance Abuse and Mental Health Services Administration (SAMHSA). Accessed June 04, 2019. http://suicidepreventionlifeline.org/.

10   "Make New Friends." Scout Songs. 2019. Accessed June 04, 2019. https://www.scoutsongs.com/lyrics/ makenewfriends.html.

11   Frost, Robert. "The Road Not Taken by Robert Frost." Poetry Foundation. 2019. Accessed June 04, 2019. https://www.poetryfoundation.org/poems/44272/ the-road-not-taken.

12   Centers for Disease Control and Prevention. "Quick Facts on the Risks of E-cigarettes for Kids, Teens, and Young Adults." CDC. March 11, 2019. Accessed June 04, 2019. https://www.cdc.gov/tobacco/basic_ information/e-cigarettes/Quick-Facts-on-the-Risks-o f-E-cigarettes-for-Kids-Teens-and-Young-Adults.html.

13   Alcoholics Anonymous. "Is A. A. for You?" AA. 2019. Accessed June 04, 2019. https://www.aa.org/pages/ en_US/is-aa-for-you.

     American Addiction Centers. "How Can You Tell If Someone Has A Drinking Problem?" Alcohol.org.

September 13, 2018. Accessed June 04, 2019. https://www.alcohol.org/faq/drinking-problem-signs/.

Centers for Disease Control and Prevention. "Fact Sheets-Binge Drinking - Alcohol." CDC. October 24, 2018. Accessed June 04, 2019. https://www.cdc.gov/alcohol/fact-sheets/binge-drinking.htm.

14 Riggs, David. "Post-Traumatic Stress Disorder." Mental Health America. May 10, 2018. Accessed June 04, 2019. https://www.mentalhealthamerica.net/conditions/post-traumatic-stress-disorder.

15 Ritvo, Eva. "The Neuroscience of Giving." *Psychology Today*. April 24, 2014. Accessed June 05, 2019. https://www.psychologytoday.com/us/blog/vitality/201404/the-neuroscience-giving.

Helpful Phone Numbers and Websites

Abuse
- National Domestic Violence Hotline 1-800-799-7233
- https://www.thehotline.org/

Alcohol
- Phone numbers to your local AA organizations on the website.
- https://www.aa.org/pages/en_US/index

Crisis Text Line
- Text HOME to 741741
- https://www.crisistextline.org/texting-in

Pornography
- Addiction Center 1-844-487-1380
- https://www.addictioncenter.com/drugs/porn-addiction/

Post-Traumatic Stress Disorder
- NAMI HelpLine at 1-800-950-NAMI (6264)
- info@nami.org
- National Alliance on Mental Illness can answer questions about PTSD or help find support and resources.

Substance Abuse and Mental Health Services Administration
- SAMHSA's National Helpline – **1-800-662-HELP (4357)**
- Free, confidential, 24/7, 365-day-a-year treatment referral and information service (in English and Spanish) for individuals and families facing mental and/or substance use disorders.
- https://www.samhsa.gov/find-help/national-helpline

Suicide
- 1-800-273-8255
- http://suicidepreventionlifeline.org/.

Tobacco/Vaping
- 1-800-QUIT-NOW (800-784-8669)
- https://smokefree.gov/

Acknowledgments

My deepest gratitude goes to my high school sweetheart who grew with me into the wonderfully content married couple we are today. Sean, you provide wisdom and calm to my mind and heart every day, and I am thankful to have you to share our empty nest.

My children also deserve a big shout out because I used all the advice in my letters on them first as they were growing up. Bless their hearts. I admire them and feel an overwhelming pride as they serve others. Zachary and Megan, you are the reason for my mantra to be nice, do good things, and make new friends!

My past students created the foundation for this book, and my Eastern Greene High School ACP classes for 2018 and 2019 were wonderful sounding boards and givers of advice when I needed direction. Many of you will find yourselves and your strengths in these pages, and I am thankful for you all.

The "Best Beta Readers Ever" awards go to Bailey Caswell, Jason Childress, Nancy Hudson, Jordyn Kieft, Kathy (and Henry) Luessow, Becky Noel, Carla Priest, and Dana Wonder. Thank you all for taking time out of your lives to help me make this dream come true. Your words of encouragement along with the awesome suggestions made me more confident in my voice for this project.

Meet the Author

Lori Vandeventer earned her Bachelor of Science in English from Indiana State University and her Master of Library Science degree from Indiana University. Lori started her career teaching English to high school students in 1990. In 2006 she became a librarian and devoted herself to collaborating with colleagues, writing curriculum and assessments, teaching  students, attending and presenting for professional development opportunities, serving as a mentor, directing a peer tutoring program, and advising honor society students.

To her delight, Lori is also teaching dual credit English courses through Indiana University and Ivy Tech Community College. As teacher and librarian, Lori considers the school system her mission field where she can serve others, and she holds a commitment to young adults and the parents, teachers, and mentors who work with them. Known as Van to her students, she continues to feel the passion and creativity involved with teaching young adults.

Lori and her husband are both committed to education, and they enjoy coming home to their Boxers, Prince and Pepper. Lori's young adult twins are also a tremendous source of love and pride as they create their way in the world.

Connect with Lori
at http://www.lorivandeventer.com today!

Meet the Publisher

Kary Oberbrunner and David Branderhorst created Author Academy Elite in 2014 rather by accident. Their clients kept asking for a program to help them write, publish, and market their books the right way.

After months of resisting, they shared a new publishing paradigm one evening in March on a private call. They had nothing built and knew it would take six months to implement that idea and create a premium experience.

Regardless of the unknowns, twenty-five aspiring authors jumped in immediately, and Author Academy Elite was born. Today, Author Academy Elite attracts hundreds of quality authors who share a mutual commitment to create vibrant businesses around their books.

Got a story inside you?
Author Academy Elite could be the right choice
for helping you write, publish, and market your book.
Discover more at https://vt226.isrefer.com/go/aaevtrng/
lorivandeventer/

⊺AUTHOR elite
ACADEMY

Become More Auspicious!

FREE GROUP ACTIVITIES GUIDE
Download detailed information about the activities described in Lori's letters to use with your group.

CONNECT TO FAITH-BASED CURRICULUM
Develop your spiritual focus with the content of *The Auspicious You* linked to Bible verses and spiritual discussion questions.

DISCOVER YOUR DESIRE TO SERVE
Engage in the 5-Day Challenge to begin serving with purpose.

CONTACT LORI VANDEVENTER
Connect with Lori! She can work with you to present a talk to your group, lead a customized workshop, or become your personal coach.

www.lorivandeventer.com

Dear Auspicious You,

What an adventure! I am so proud of the way you are embracing life as you move into these new roles. You are no longer waiting to see what kinds of freedoms await you. Now, you are making choices that will determine your own future. You _are_ gaining new responsibility every day, but you are ready to handle the tasks ahead of you.

I know you face big decisions. You feel like the rest of your life hangs in the balance of college, major, internships, and your GPA. You are wise to recognize the importance of these parts of your life. However, you are more than the sum of your student identity. Remember your plan to explore life's adventures, serve others, and laugh. You have the potential to continually create a difference in the world, and I'm excited to see where your choices take you. Enjoy the journey as you go!

♡ Van